MADDALENA CARUSO
LOVE
ITALIAN FOOD

Recipes for Friends and Family from a Home in Asolo

jacqui
small

First published in 2012 by
Jacqui Small LLP
An imprint of Aurum Press
7 Greenland Street
London NW1 0ND

Text copyright © 2012
Design and layout copyright
© Jacqui Small 2012

The author's moral rights
have been asserted.

Publisher: Jacqui Small
Managing Editor: Kerenza Swift
Designer: Lawrence Morton
Editor: Hilary Mandleberg
Translators: Lindy Wildsmith
   and Eva Barraclough
Production: Peter Colley

ISBN: 978 1 906417 75 8

A catalogue record for this
book is available from the
British Library.

2014 2013 2012
10 9 8 7 6 5 4 3 2 1

Printed in China

How I got here is a simple story of obstinate passion and no half measures. I am only 35 years old, yet the memories of my first ventures in the kitchen seem lost in the mists of time. At the beginning, my forays into cooking were a rather messy business and the results were rough and ready, almost as though I was approaching the subject without much concern as to the outcome. Later on, as I became aware that cooking was developing into an essential expression of my creativity, I began to understand how important it was going to be to my life. My style of cooking is unpredictable; it may veer this way and that or follow a steady course, but I always have the same goal in my sights – to produce simple dishes that follow the changing seasons and cock a snook at tradition, while remaining true to my own nature. I combine flavours guided by my instinct. Every now and then I add a pinch of reason – but never too much. I sincerely hope that through the pages of this book – which form my personal 'manifesto' – you will pay me a visit once, ten times or a hundred times. It will be exciting to guide you through the places I adore, to tell you what I love to cook and why, to involve you in my cooking and then to lead you into the garden to gather the best of the season's produce and the first fruits of the orchard. I hope you will come to feel, as I do, that serving up good food is a wonderful way to care for the people we love and gives us the perfect opportunity to share precious time with them when, sadly, spending time together is becoming more of a rarity in modern life. The journey I have been on would not have been possible without the staunch support of the many people who have unstintingly trusted in my abilities and have imbued me with the overwhelming passion needed for this great venture. And now it is time to go. The four seasons await us, along with very many tasty recipes.

SPRING

Spring cooking

Spring arrives and advances, always the same, yet always new.

It is everywhere: in the colour of the sky, in the gentle but vivacious warmth of the sun, amid the tree branches, in the flowery fields and in the orchards where the first buds are appearing. The house where I live and its surrounding region have taught me what it means to live in tune with the seasons, but spring is probably the season closest to my heart and the one I most eagerly await. In the kitchen there is the longing for new, fresh produce: broad beans, peas, artichokes, asparagus and tomatoes are some of those that embellish the spring table and grace the first meals *al fresco*. Ensuring that the flavours are light, making the dishes virtual palettes of brilliant colour and respecting the ingredients are all it takes to prepare these young, tender vegetables. One of my culinary precepts is that the less produce is 'manipulated' the better. I have always been a firm believer that good-quality produce, eaten in the right season, should not be de-naturalized by elaborate cooking processes, over-fanciful combinations or excessively invasive condiments. I always prefer a dish that brings together the honest taste of the soil, good texture and a harmony of colours.

Carta musica con asparagi verdi, fonduta di piselli e pecorino
Pane carasau with asparagus, pea fondue and pecorino

This recipe uses *pane carasau*, the typical bread of Sardinia. If you can find *guttiàu*, or 'dripping', *pane carasau*, sprinkle with a few drops of extra virgin olive oil and a pinch of salt, and heat in a 160°C (325°F/Gas 3) oven for 5 minutes before using. Alternatively, use the classic *pane carasau* and simply season lightly with salt and oil.

Serves 6

1kg (2lb) green asparagus spears

2–3 tbsp extra virgin olive oil, plus extra to drizzle

800g (1½lb/5 cups) peas, freshly picked, shelled, washed and dried

80g (3oz/1 cup) grated Pecorino Romano cheese (not too mature [sharp])

3–5 sheets of *pane carasau*, lightly seasoned with salt and a little extra virgin olive oil

salt and freshly ground black pepper

Wash the asparagus, then bend each spear. The spear should snap easily at the point where the woody part begins. Discard the tough, woody base. Half-fill a tall narrow saucepan with salted water and bring to the boil.

Stand the asparagus spears in the saucepan with their tips just above the boiling salted water and cook for about 8 minutes, or until the stems are tender but the tips are still crispy. Remove from the water, drain and leave to cool on paper towels.

Meanwhile, heat the olive oil in a pan over a medium heat, add the peas and salt to taste, reduce the heat and cook for about 15 minutes. Stir occasionally and add a little water if the peas get too dry.

Whizz the well-cooked peas in a blender to make a smooth cream. Add a drizzle of olive oil, the Pecorino Romano cheese and pepper to taste. Mix well.

Slice the cooled asparagus spears lengthways, then carefully spread 1 sheet of *pane carasau* with the pea mixture. Lay 7–9 spears of asparagus on top in a fan, with the tips towards the outside. Repeat with more layers of *pane carasau*, the pea mixture and asparagus to create a layered 'torta'. Finish with a layer of the pea mixture. Serve warm.

Mezzi paccheri con fave, pecorino e guanciale
Mezzi paccheri with broad beans, pecorino and guanciale

This is a popular dish both in Lazio and in Tuscany but I love it here in the Veneto when the first young tender broad (fava) beans of spring appear on the greengrocers' stalls.

Serves 6

1 tbsp extra virgin olive oil, plus extra to drizzle

3 thick slices of aged guanciale (unsmoked bacon made from pig's cheek) or pancetta, cut into thin strips

100ml (3½fl oz/scant ½ cup) light vegetable stock

1 spring onion (scallion), thinly sliced

50ml (2fl oz/scant ¼ cup) dry white wine

200g (7oz/1⅓ cups) broad (fava) beans, shelled

600g (1¼lb/1⅓cups) mezzi paccheri (or other short pasta such as penne, orecchiette, fusilli)

70g (scant 3oz/scant 1 cup) grated Pecorino Romano cheese or Pecorino Sardo cheese

salt and freshly ground black pepper

Heat the olive oil in a deep pan over a medium heat. Add the guanciale or pancetta and fry for 3 minutes, until golden and crispy but not dry.

Meanwhile, bring the stock to the boil in another pan.

Add the sliced spring onion (scallion) to the guanciale or pancetta, mix gently, then add the wine. Cook for 2–3 minutes, until the wine has evaporated, then add the broad (fava) beans and the boiling stock and continue to cook for 7–8 minutes. Add salt to taste, taking into account the saltiness of the guanciale or pancetta.

Meanwhile, bring a large pan of salted water to the boil. Add the pasta, reduce the heat and cook for 11–13 minutes, until al dente, then drain.

Tip the pasta into the pan containing the guanciale or pancetta and the broad (fava) beans and mix well. Add the grated cheese, pepper to taste and a drizzle of olive oil. Stir well and serve immediately.

Acknowledgements

I would like to thank the following people and businesses for helping me to make the pages of this book even more beautiful:

Ceramica Artistica Solimene
Via Madonna degli Angeli 7
84019 Vietri sul mare
www.solimene.com

Jesurum
Calle Larga XXII Marzo San Marco
2401
Venezia
www.jesurum.it

Fiorirà un Giardino
Via Galileo galilei 10
34042 Buttrio Udine
www.fioriraungiardino.com

Primizie Moreno Snc di Grigoletto
Moreno & C.
Corte Dei Berri 2
36061 Bassano del Grappa (VI)

Asolo Kilim di Damiano Pellizzari
Via Marconi 132
31011 Asolo

Galleria Asolana Preziosi e
Antichità, di Gianna Vettorato
Via Browning 163
31011 Asolo

Index

Crema ai fiori d'arancio con datteri
Orange-flower custard with dates

The best moments are when I look out over the Mediterranean and breathe deeply: I smell fragrances and revisit colours, and the sensation of travelling resurfaces powerfully. This custard is reminiscent of the refined, soft aroma of some of the sumptuous sweets I have eaten under African skies. Moments of nostalgia.

Serves 6

600ml (1 pint/2½ cups) milk

150g (5oz/scant ¾ cup) caster (superfine) sugar

3 egg yolks

1 egg

4 tbsp orange-flower water

20 dates, to serve

Put the milk and 125g (4oz/generous ½ cup) of the sugar in a saucepan over a medium heat. As soon as the milk reaches boiling point, turn off the heat and leave to cool.

Meanwhile, beat the egg yolks and the whole egg together in a bowl with the remaining sugar, then add the orange-flower water followed by the cooled milk. Mix well.

Put the mixture back in the pan over a low heat. Continue to cook for about 10 minutes, stirring continuously, until the custard starts to thicken and coats the back of the spoon. Do not allow the custard to boil at any point. Serve warm or cold with the dates on the side.

Macedonia di frutti invernali con zafferano e vaniglia
Winter fruit salad with saffron and vanilla

This salad of tasty, fragrant, barely cooked winter fruits is an unusual way to conclude any meal. My only recommendation is that you choose fruit not only of the best-quality but also of the right dimensions – it will look its best with whole pieces of fruit.

Serves 6

4 small firm pears

5 small apples

small bunch of green grapes

small bunch of black grapes

1 tbsp extra virgin olive oil

2 tbsp honey

1 Bourbon vanilla pod (bean), slit lengthways

3 tbsp Armagnac

pinch of saffron threads

Prepare the fruit. Cut up the pears and apples, some in half, some in quarters. Do not peel or core. Separate the grapes. Put the olive oil in a non-stick frying pan over a low heat, add the honey and cook until melted, then add the vanilla pod (bean). Continue to cook for 2–3 minutes, until the honey starts to caramelize, then add the fruit. Increase the heat, shake the pan vigorously for a second or two, then add the Armagnac and continue to cook until this has evaporated. Finally, add the saffron. Reduce the heat and cook for 5–7 minutes more, until the fruit is completely caramelized and soft. The syrup should remain soft, too. Remove the vanilla pod (bean) and serve warm.

Torta di amaretti, pere e mele
Apple and pear amaretti torta

There are many different amaretti, but I always stick to the classic variety – hard and crunchy with a well-balanced proportion of sweet and bitter almonds. Amaretti go perfectly with fruit. Here I have paired them with winter fruit, but they are also extraordinarily good crumbled on top of an aromatic peach salad.

Serves 6–8

knob of unsalted butter, for greasing

flour, for dusting

2 pears

2 apples

220g (7½oz) amaretti biscuits (cookies)

7 eggs, separated

200g (7oz/scant 1 cup) caster (superfine) sugar

75g (3oz/1 cup) dry white breadcrumbs

75ml (3fl oz/scant ⅓ cup) Marsala Cremovo wine

zest of 1 lemon, finely grated

1 heaped tsp baking powder

Preheat the oven to 180°C (350°F/Gas 4) and lightly grease and flour a 25cm (10in) diameter cake tin (pan). Peel the pears and apples and cut into quarters, discarding the cores, then cut into slices lengthways. Line the base of the tin (pan) with the apples and the sides of the tin (pan) with the pears.

Put the amaretti in a blender and grind them to crumbs. Beat the egg yolks with the sugar in one bowl and whisk the egg whites until stiff in another. Carefully fold the egg whites into the egg yolk mixture. Fold in the crumbed amaretti and the breadcrumbs, then moisten the mixture with the Marsala. Add the grated lemon zest and finally the baking powder.

Mix well, then pour the mixture into the fruit-lined cake tin (pan). Place in the preheated oven and cook for 40 minutes. After this time, insert a cocktail stick (toothpick) in the centre – it should come out perfectly dry. Remove the torta from the oven and leave to cool. Remove from the tin (pan) before serving.

Vitello in salsa gremolada
Veal with gremolada sauce

Gremolada sauce typically accompanies Milanese ossobuco, which, when well prepared, is a delicacy fit for grand gourmets. Consequently, when we are all together for Sunday lunch, I use this sauce to scent the slowly and carefully cooked veal rump. The meat is perfect even when just slightly warm.

Serves 6

50g (2oz/scant ¼ cup) unsalted butter

1 small onion, finely chopped

875g (1¾lb) topside (round) of veal

100ml (3½fl oz/scant ½ cup) dry white wine

100ml (3½fl oz/scant ½ cup) beef stock

salt and freshly ground black pepper

for the gremolada sauce

½ large garlic clove, peeled

handful of flat-leaf parsley

zest of 1 small lemon, finely grated

Heat the butter in a large heavy-based pan over a low heat, add the chopped onion and cook for 10 minutes until just golden brown.

Increase the heat, add the piece of veal and brown all over, taking care not to burn the onion. Add the wine and cook for 7 minutes more, until the wine has evaporated. Add the stock and salt and pepper to taste, reduce the heat, cover the pan and cook for 1 hour more, turning the meat from time to time, until the meat is tender and the liquid has turned to sauce.

Meanwhile, make the gremolada sauce. Chop the garlic and parsley very finely, add the finely grated lemon zest and mix together.

When the meat is ready, spread the gremolada on top and mix it into the pan juices. To serve, cut the meat into slices and accompany with plenty of sauce.

Lasagne con ragout di lepre
Lasagne with hare sauce

This is the classic 'Italian style' lasagne but with a hare-based ragoût. All the regions of Italy have traditional pasta or lasagne recipes made with game. Although hare is probably the kind most commonly used, boar, duck, pheasant, roebuck and venison all provide the basis for the best ragoûts I have ever eaten.

Serves 6

for the hare sauce

1kg (2lb) hare, skinned, removed from the bone and cut into pieces

200ml (7fl oz/generous ¾ cup) full-bodied red wine

3–4 juniper berries, crushed

1 onion, peeled

1 carrot, peeled

1 celery stick, trimmed

1 garlic clove, peeled and halved

2 tbsp extra virgin olive oil

75ml (3fl oz/scant ⅓ cup) tomato passata

100ml (3½fl oz/scant ½ cup) beef stock

1 sprig of rosemary

salt and freshly ground black pepper

for the pasta

500g (1lb/3⅓ cups) 00 flour, sifted, plus extra for dusting

5 eggs

pinch of salt

for the white sauce

500ml (17fl oz/2 cups) milk

60g (2½oz/¼ cup) unsalted butter, plus extra for greasing and dotting

50g (2oz/⅓ cup) 00 flour

pinch of nutmeg

75g (3oz/scant 1 cup) grated Parmesan cheese

salt and freshly ground black pepper

First, make the hare sauce. Put the pieces of hare in a bowl with 100ml (3½fl oz/scant ½ cup) of the wine and the crushed juniper berries. Cover with clingfilm (plastic wrap) and leave to marinate in the refrigerator for 3 hours.

Meanwhile, chop the onion, carrot and celery together finely. Heat the olive oil in a flameproof casserole dish over a medium heat, add the chopped vegetables and garlic and cook for 7–8 minutes, stirring occasionally, until soft.

Drain the pieces of marinated hare and pat dry with paper towels. Add them to the casserole dish and cook for 10 minutes, until the hare is slightly golden. Increase the heat, add the remaining wine and season to taste with the salt and pepper, then continue to cook until the wine has evaporated. Mix together the tomato passata and stock, add to the casserole dish and cook for 20 minutes more, until the meat starts to fall away from the bones.

Remove the pieces of hare with a slotted spoon, cut the meat off the bones, then return the meat to the casserole dish. Add the rosemary and cook over a low heat for 5–7 minutes, until all the ingredients are well combined and the sauce is creamy. Remove from the heat, leave to cool and set aside.

Next, make the pasta. Heap the flour on a work surface, make a well in the centre and add the eggs and salt. Mix together using the tips of your fingers and incorporating the flour a little at a time. Knead the dough energetically for 15–20 minutes until it becomes smooth, stretchy and really firm. Wrap the dough in a clean cloth and leave to rest in a cool place for 30 minutes.

To make sheets of lasagne with a pasta-making machine, set the rollers to their widest position and dust lightly with flour. Take a handful of dough and feed it through the rollers. Repeat several times, each time setting the rollers closer together until you have a very thin sheet. Cut into pieces measuring about 10 x 15cm (4 x 6in). Bring a pan of salted water to the boil over a high heat, add the lasagne and cook for 3–4 minutes, until very al dente. Drain and set aside.

Finally, make the white sauce. Heat the milk in a saucepan over a low heat. Melt the butter in another saucepan over a low heat, stir in the flour and mix well until thickened and the butter is completely absorbed by the flour. Add the hot milk, salt, nutmeg and a dusting of pepper. Increase the heat slightly and bring to the boil, stirring all the time. Reduce the heat and simmer for 2–3 minutes. Do not overcook as the sauce should be quite runny.

To assemble the lasagne, preheat the oven to 180°C (350°F/Gas 4). Grease an ovenproof dish, about 10cm (4in) deep, cover the base with a layer of lasagne, then pour a ladleful of hare sauce over the pasta – it does not have to cover the lasagne completely.

Spread some white sauce on top of the hare sauce, then add a sprinkling of Parmesan cheese. Cover with another layer of lasagne and repeat the other layers until all the pasta has been used up. Finish with a sprinkling of Parmesan, then dot with butter. Place in the preheated oven and cook for 30 minutes, until the top is golden brown. Remove from the oven and serve immediately.

Pan brioché con pâté di selvaggina e frutta secca
Homemade brioche with game and dried fruit pâté

Everyone should try to make brioche at least once in a lifetime. The aroma that emerges from the oven in the last ten minutes makes all the effort worthwhile. Just slightly sweet, brioche is a perfect accompaniment to a delicate but full-flavoured game pâté, full of subtle overtones, like this one.

Serves 6

for the pâté

1 tbsp dried cranberries

1 tbsp dried apricots

1 tbsp dates

1 tbsp dried figs

1 tbsp walnuts, shelled

100ml (3½fl oz/scant ½ cup) fortified wine (such as Marsala)

175g (6oz) bought, good-quality game pâté

for the brioche

25g (1oz) fresh brewer's yeast

100ml (3½fl oz/scant ½ cup) full-cream (whole) milk, warm

500g (1lb/3⅓ cups) 00 flour, finely sifted, plus extra for dusting

pinch of salt

2 tbsp caster (superfine) sugar

3 eggs

150g (5oz/scant ⅔ cup) unsalted butter, softened and diced, plus extra for greasing

lightly beaten egg, to glaze

First make the pâté. Chop the dried fruit and walnuts finely and place in a bowl with the wine. Put in the refrigerator for 1 hour to soak, then squeeze dry and mix into the pâté. Press into 6 individual serving dishes, cover with clingfilm (plastic wrap) and keep in the refrigerator until ready to serve.

Next, make the brioche. In a large bowl, dissolve the yeast in the warm milk, then add 125g (4oz/generous ¾ cup) of the flour and mix well. Knead the dough in the bowl, ensuring it remains soft, then shape it into a ball. Cut a cross in the top, wrap in a clean cloth and leave to prove in a warm place for 45 minutes, until the dough has doubled in size.

Meanwhile, mix the remaining flour with the salt and sugar and tip in a mound on a lightly floured surface. Add the eggs and knead together well. Add the softened butter and carry on kneading until the dough is smooth and stretchy. Work this piece of dough into the piece that has now doubled in size. Knead the pieces energetically together on the work surface, folding and dividing them, then kneading them together again until the dough is soft and stretchy. Wrap in a lightly floured clean cloth and leave to prove for 2 hours in a warm place.

After this time, put the dough back on the work surface and knead again for a few minutes, then cover with the cloth again and leave somewhere cool for a few hours, or even overnight if it suits you.

Preheat the oven to 200°C (400°F/Gas 6) and grease a 26 x 10 x 7.5cm (10½ x 4 x 3¼in) cake tin (pan). Put the dough in the tin (pan) and brush the surface with the beaten egg. Place in the preheated oven and cook for 25–30 minutes, until the dough has risen, the surface is golden and the inside is cooked when tested with a cocktail stick (toothpick).

Serve the game and dried fruit pâté with slices of warm brioche.

Sunday lunch is a dear tradition in Italian families; it captures

the sense of togetherness which these days is becoming more of a rarity. At home I always count on my husband, his two sons, Michele and Nicola, and my own son, Nicolò. Sometimes we also have friends round and even the grandparents, when we can drag them away from Venetian life. I don't impose a menu on Sundays, but like everyone to choose from the selection of simple dishes I have prepared. Normally the lasagne are made with Nicolò in mind, while the stronger tastes, like the veal with gremolada sauce, are a tribute to my husband. These are peaceful hours spent in quiet harmony: we joke, we argue and just let time go quietly by. We know full well that Monday is inevitable but we can perhaps delude ourselves into thinking that tomorrow will be another Sunday and that we shall all be here again enjoying good food and good company.

Uova fritte con croste di polenta al rosmarino e crema di finocchi
Fried eggs, crunchy rosemary polenta fingers and creamed fennel

Simple dishes, although served in an original way, are those that really make me happy. I am always amazed to realize that eggs and polenta are not only truly good but are also perfect on a Sunday table set for family and friends. This is a great recipe for kids, who will dip the polenta in the yolks and wolf it down. Guaranteed.

Serves 6

2 tbsp extra virgin olive oil

6 large fresh eggs

salt

for the polenta fingers

500g (1lb/3 cups) instant polenta (cornmeal)

40g (1½oz/scant ¼ cup) unsalted butter, plus extra for greasing

100g (3½oz/generous ½ cup) polenta (cornmeal) flour, plus extra for dusting

1 egg, lightly beaten

6 sprigs of rosemary

salt

for the creamed fennel

1kg (2lb) fennel

40g (1½oz/scant ¼ cup) unsalted butter

100ml (3½fl oz/scant ½ cup) full-cream (whole) milk

a few rosemary leaves, finely chopped

piece of lemon zest, finely grated

salt and freshly ground black pepper

Make the polenta fingers. Preheat the oven to 200°C (400°F/Gas 6). Make 1.5 litres (2½ pints/6⅓ cups) polenta (cornmeal), following the packet instructions. Put the prepared polenta (cornmeal) into a well-greased 28 x 15cm (11 x 6in) ovenproof dish and leave the polenta (cornmeal) to cool and set firm.

Dust a work surface with polenta (cornmeal) flour, turn the polenta out onto it and cut it into 24 fingers. Dip each finger in the lightly beaten egg and then in the remaining polenta (cornmeal) flour. Tie the polenta fingers up in fours with string, slipping a sprig of rosemary under the string. Arrange in a roasting tin (pan), add a few dots of butter and sprinkle lightly with salt. Place in the preheated oven and cook for 25–30 minutes, or until crisp.

Meanwhile, make the creamed fennel. Trim the fennel and cut into small pieces. Melt the butter in a saucepan over a low heat, add the fennel and cook for 15 minutes, until tender. Season with salt and pepper.

Bring the milk to the boil in another pan over a medium heat, then add to the pan with the fennel. Cook for 7 minutes more, until the fennel is really creamy. Add the rosemary leaves and lemon zest, then set aside.

Heat the olive oil in a non-stick frying pan over a medium heat. Carefully break the eggs into the pan one at a time and cook for 3 minutes, until the whites are set but the yolks are still runny and bright yellow. When the eggs are ready, add salt to taste and use a pastry (cookie) cutter to trim the whites into circles, making sure the yolks are in the middle with just a small amount of white all around.

To serve, put a fried egg on each plate accompanied by the crispy polenta fingers and the creamed fennel.

Sunday lunch

Vellutate di cavolo rosso, bianco e verde
Tricolor cream of brassica soups

More than a dish, this is an entire colour palette that is bound to elicit a response! The purple part has a full, slightly peppery flavour without being aggressive. The white and green, in contrast, are incredibly delicate, while the nutmeg adds a fanciful, warm, sweet note. Best served as a light appetizer.

Serves 6

for the purple soup

2 tbsp extra virgin olive oil

½ red onion, thinly sliced

1 garlic clove, halved

1 red cabbage, trimmed, halved, cored and thinly sliced

375g (12oz) purple potatoes, peeled and diced

1 litre (1¾ pints/4 cups) vegetable stock, boiling

salt

cauliflower florets, to garnish

Heat the olive oil in a large heavy-based pan over a medium heat, add the onion and garlic, reduce the heat and cook for 3 minutes, stirring frequently, until softened.

Add the cabbage and potatoes, the hot vegetable stock and salt to taste. Cook for 20 minutes, stirring occasionally, until the vegetables are tender. Transfer to a blender and whizz until smooth. Add more salt if necessary. Serve very hot, garnished with cauliflower florets.

for the white or green soup

1 large cauliflower (for the white soup) or 1 head of Romanesco broccoli (for the green soup), cut into pieces

3 potatoes, peeled and diced

750ml (1¼ pints/3 cups) full-cream (whole) milk

2 pinches each of nutmeg, salt and freshly ground black pepper

2 tbsp sour cream

to garnish

Romanesco broccoli florets or red cabbage, finely sliced

Bring a large pan of salted water to the boil over a high heat, add the prepared cauliflower (or broccoli) and the potatoes, reduce the heat and cook for 15 minutes, until the vegetables are tender. Drain and put them through a food mill.

Meanwhile, pour the milk into a medium heavy-based pan, add the nutmeg, salt and pepper and bring to the boil over a medium heat.

Stir the cauliflower (or broccoli) and potato purée into the pan of hot milk, together with the sour cream. Bring back to the boil and cook for 3 minutes, adding a little water to thin if necessary. Serve very hot. Garnish the white soup with florets of Romanesco broccoli and the green soup with some finely sliced red cabbage.

Cime di rapa ripassate con pane fritto
Sprouting broccoli with fried breadcrumbs

I have done no more than slip a little extra garlic into this typical recipe from Puglia, which is perhaps the best way to enjoy the pungent and slightly bitter-tasting broccoli. I prefer to parboil the broccoli so it retains its characteristic flavour, but if you prefer a sweeter taste, boil it fully.

Serves 6

1kg (2lb) sprouting broccoli, cut into small pieces, tough stalks discarded

2 tbsp extra virgin olive oil

1 garlic clove, peeled

1 hot chilli pepper

75g (3oz/1 cup) fresh white breadcrumbs

Bring a pan of salted water to the boil over a high heat, add the pieces of broccoli and cook for 7 minutes, or until cooked but still crisp. Drain well and set aside.

Heat half the olive oil in a frying pan over a high heat, add the whole garlic and whole chilli and cook for 5–6 minutes, shaking the pan frequently. Transfer to a serving plate and leave to rest for a few minutes.

Meanwhile, heat the remaining olive oil in the same pan for a few seconds, then add the breadcrumbs and fry quickly until golden brown, stirring frequently to ensure they do not burn. To serve, sprinkle the fried breadcrumbs over the sprouting broccoli.

Insalata croccante di broccolo romanesco
Crispy broccoli salad

A sweet taste, a beautiful bright green colour and a fascinating, remarkably regular shape are just some of the elements that make this crunchy salad truly good and appetizing. Enjoy its rich, fragrant flavour, whether on the side or on its own, in almost religious silence.

Serves 6

1½ tbsp pine nuts

2 heads of Romanesco broccoli or 2 heads of regular broccoli, about 1kg (2lb) total

1 tbsp extra virgin olive oil

1 garlic clove, unpeeled

pinch of chilli (dried red pepper) flakes (optional)

1½ tbsp raisins, soaked in cold water for 20 minutes, then drained and dried

3 anchovies in oil, finely chopped

salt

Heat a dry frying pan over a medium heat, add the pine nuts and toast them, stirring continuously to ensure they do not burn. Set aside.

Trim the broccoli, reserving the green florets and discarding the stem. Bring a pan of salted water to the boil over a high heat, add the broccoli florets, reduce the heat and cook for 5 minutes. Drain and immerse briefly in ice-cold water to help retain the colour. Drain again and dry well with paper towels.

Heat the olive oil in a frying pan over a medium heat, add the garlic clove and chilli, if using, and cook for 1 minute, stirring, to allow the flavours to permeate the oil. Add the drained broccoli and mix gently. Cook for 4 minutes, stirring occasionally, then add the raisins and toasted pine nuts. Mix carefully, add the anchovies, then add salt to taste and cook for 2–3 minutes more.

Cotechino con fagioli e verza
Cotechino sausage with beans and cabbage

This good, honest dish has all the ingredients needed to bring many dear friends together around the table. Cotechino is made of pork meat, fat and rind (*cotenna*). Because of the *cotenna*, the sausage is technically defined as 'poor'. Take note that cotechino should be brought to the boil very slowly, after which the water should barely simmer.

Serves 6

175g (6oz/generous ¾ cup) dried cannellini beans soaked overnight in cold water and rinsed

1 bay leaf

2 cotechino sausages

1 Savoy cabbage

1 shallot

1 tbsp extra virgin olive oil

80–100ml (3–3½fl oz/scant ⅓–scant ½ cup) water

2 tbsp red wine vinegar

salt and freshly ground black pepper

Put the soaked and rinsed cannellini beans in a large saucepan, cover with cold water, add a bay leaf and bring to the boil over a low heat. Simmer for 1 hour, or until the beans are very soft. Add a pinch of salt towards the end of the cooking time. Drain and set aside.

Prick the cotechino sausages with a fork in several places and put in a saucepan with just enough water to cover. Bring to the boil slowly, then simmer for 2½ hours, until the sausage is cooked.

Meanwhile, trim the cabbage and cut into thick slices and peel the shallot and chop finely. Heat the olive oil in a large saucepan over a medium heat, add the shallot and cook, stirring occasionally, for 2–3 minutes until soft. Add the cooked cannellini beans and the water, then cook until the water has almost evaporated. Add the cabbage then the vinegar and cook until the vinegar has evaporated. Add salt and pepper to taste, stir, then cook for 15 minutes more, or until the cabbage is tender. Add some water if the mixture is too thick.

To serve, cut the cotechino into slices with its skin still on and serve with the warm cannellini beans and cabbage.

Minestra di fagiano e verza
Pheasant and cabbage soup

This recipe was born on a cold winter afternoon when I was getting ready to seat 14 people for dinner. The lean, firm pheasant meat helps to make the soup a complete dish, while the use of cabbage gives it a hearty flavour. This is now a winter classic in our home.

Serves 6

1 oven-ready pheasant, about 1.2kg (2½lb)

1 carrot

2 celery sticks

2 onions, 1 peeled and stuck with 3 cloves and 1 peeled and finely sliced

2 tbsp extra virgin olive oil

4–5 black peppercorns

3–4 juniper berries

1 cabbage, trimmed, cored and finely sliced

75ml (3fl oz/scant ⅓ cup) dry white wine

salt and freshly ground black pepper

Put the pheasant in a large pan with the carrot, celery and the onion stuck with cloves. Add just enough cold water to cover, then bring to the boil over a medium heat. Cook for 1½ hours, until the meat comes away from the bones easily. Remove the pheasant from the pan and leave to cool. Strain the stock into a clean pan and keep hot over a medium heat.

When the pheasant is cool enough to handle, take all the meat off the bone and cut into smallish, even-sized pieces. Set aside.

Heat the olive oil in a large deep pan over a medium heat, add the sliced onion, reduce the heat and fry for 2–3 minutes, until soft. Add the peppercorns and juniper berries, stir and continue to cook for 1 minute. Add the prepared pheasant meat and cabbage and stir to combine all the ingredients. Add the wine and continue to cook until it has evaporated. Add 2 pinches of salt, then taste, adding more salt if necessary. Cook for 1–2 minutes more, until the cabbage has wilted and is tender, then add 1.2 litres (2 pints/5 cups) of the boiling hot, strained stock. If the flavour of the stock is too intense, dilute with water by one-third. Continue to cook over a medium heat for 25–30 minutes. Serve the soup steaming hot with a grinding of black pepper.

Ravioli di cernia con fonduta di cavolo rosso
Fish ravioli with red cabbage purée

Grouper is extraordinarily good and versatile. Its exquisite firm flesh provides the inspiration for the delicate but striking filling for these ravioli, which I then dress with the red cabbage purée. Given the natural light pungency of the purée, it proves the perfect accompaniment.

Serves 6

extra virgin olive oil, to drizzle

for the pasta

400g (13oz/2⅔ cups) 00 flour, sifted

4 very fresh eggs, plus 1 extra egg to seal the ravioli

pinch of salt

for the filling

1 celery stick

1 carrot

1 small onion

500g (1lb) grouper fillets or other firm-fleshed fish such as sea bass

1 sprig of parsley

1 tbsp extra virgin olive oil

250g (8oz/1¼ cups) ricotta cheese

2 tbsp grated Parmesan cheese

salt and freshly ground black pepper

for the purée

3 tbsp extra virgin olive oil

1 garlic clove, peeled and halved

4 salted anchovies

1 red cabbage, trimmed and thinly sliced

500ml (17fl oz/2 cups) vegetable stock

salt and freshly ground black pepper

Start by making the pasta. Heap the flour on a work surface, make a well in the centre and add the eggs one at a time with the salt. Using your fingers like a paddle, first break up the eggs, then mix the flour into the eggs a little at a time. Once the flour and the eggs are combined, knead the dough energetically for 15–20 minutes until soft, smooth and springy. Work into a ball, wrap in clingfilm (plastic wrap) and leave to rest in a cool place for 30 minutes.

Meanwhile, prepare the filling. Trim the celery and peel the carrot and onion. Cut the vegetables into pieces and put in a saucepan, cover with water and bring to the boil over a high heat. Cook for 30 minutes, then discard the vegetables and strain the stock through a fine sieve. Return the stock to the heat and when it comes back to the boil, reduce the heat and add the fish. Simmer gently for 10 minutes, then remove the fish from the stock. The fillets should stay whole and the flesh should be firm and white. Leave to cool.

Wash and dry the parsley, slice it thinly, then add to the cooled fish with the olive oil, a pinch of salt and a grinding of black pepper. Mix all the ingredients together well. Finally stir in the ricotta and Parmesan cheese and mix until smooth.

Divide the pasta into 2 balls and roll each out on a lightly floured surface to a thickness of 3mm (⅛in). Spoon small heaps of the fish mixture over 1 sheet of pasta at 2.5cm (1in) intervals. Brush with lightly beaten egg and cover with the second sheet of pasta, pressing down well around the heaps of filling with the fingertips to ensure that the 2 sheets stick together well. Cut the ravioli using a ravioli cutter.

To make the purée, heat the olive oil in a saucepan over a low heat, add the garlic and the anchovies and cook for 5 minutes, until the anchovies have disintegrated. Do not let the garlic burn. Add the red cabbage and cook for 10 minutes, stirring occasionally, until it takes on the flavour of the garlic and the anchovies.

Meanwhile, heat the stock in a pan over a medium heat and when the cabbage starts to soften, add a ladle of stock. Continue to cook and as the stock evaporates, add another ladle, continuing in this way for 15 minutes. Add the remaining stock, then blend with a hand-blender. Add salt to taste and a grinding of black pepper.

Shortly before you are ready to serve the ravioli, bring a large pan of salted water to the boil over a high heat, add the ravioli and cook for 4–5 minutes. Remove with a slotted spoon and arrange on plates on top of a bed of 2–3 heaped tbsp of the hot red cabbage purée. Garnish with a few drops of purée and a drizzle of olive oil. Serve immediately.

Zuppa di farro e cavolo nero
Cavolo nero and spelt soup

Although cavolo nero is now well known everywhere, it is in Italy that it really forms part of the culinary tradition of some regions like Tuscany, where *ribollita* soup is justly famous. Mine is a lighter version of this soup whose origins are lost in the mists of time.

Serves 6

100g (3½oz/½ cup) dried cannellini beans, soaked overnight in cold water and rinsed

2 bay leaves

200g (7oz/scant 1¼ cups) spelt

1 large potato

1 onion

1 celery stick

1 carrot

500g (1lb) cavolo nero

4 tbsp extra virgin olive oil

1.5 litres (2½ pints/6⅓ cups) vegetable stock

salt and freshly ground black pepper

Put the soaked and rinsed cannellini beans in a pan of salted water with the bay leaves and bring to the boil, then reduce the heat and simmer for about 1 hour, or until really tender. Drain and set aside.

Meanwhile, soak the spelt for 2 hours in cold water, then strain. Put in a pan of lightly salted water and bring to the boil, then reduce the heat and simmer for 40 minutes. Drain and set aside.

Peel the potato and cut into cubes. Peel and chop the onion. Peel the celery and carrot and dice finely. Wash and pick over the cavolo nero, then shred it.

Heat the olive oil in a heavy-based pan over a low heat, add the prepared vegetables and cook for 7 minutes, or until they start to soften. Meanwhile, bring the stock to the boil in a separate pan.

Add the reserved beans and spelt to the vegetables and stir for a few minutes to allow the flavours to come together. Add the boiling stock and salt and pepper to taste, then cook for about 45 minutes over a low heat. Serve the soup piping hot.

I have had to temper the slight aversion I used to feel with respect to cabbages of all species, shapes and colours. It somewhat conditioned my culinary range and was attributable, in part, to a miscalculation made one year in my yield–seeds–crop rotation equation. As a result of this miscalculation, my orchard became a sort of cabbage production line and the obvious consequence was that I had to employ all my culinary skills to create recipes based on cabbage and more cabbage. Some, such as the pheasant and cabbage soup or the fish ravioli with red cabbage purée, have proved that they have true, lasting merit and so they have become part of my personal culinary tradition. The various different types of cabbage and broccoli are eaten throughout the whole of Italy and have an established presence in the gastronomy of every region from Friuli Venezia Giulia to Lombardy, from Veneto to Tuscany, down to Lazio and finally to Puglia and Sicily. Moreover, they are all highly decorative and when afforded a leading role in any setting, will always elicit joyful surprise.

Brandade di cavolo bianco e merluzzo con fogli di verza fritte
Cod and cauliflower brandade with fried cabbage leaves

I must have learned about the classic 'brandade' donkey's years ago. This version is finer and more delicate than the classic because instead of using large amounts of extra virgin olive oil, I have almost totally replaced it with milk and a little cream.

Serves 6

150g (5oz) potatoes

300g (10oz) cauliflower florets

6 large cabbage leaves

70ml (scant 3fl oz/generous ¼ cup) extra virgin olive oil, plus extra for brushing

500g (1lb) cod fillet

1 litre (1¾ pints/4 cups) milk

100ml (3½fl oz/scant ½ cup) single (light) cream

2 sprigs of thyme

salt

Wash, peel and slice the potatoes, then put them in a bowl and cover with cold water. Bring a pan of salted water to the boil over a high heat, add the cauliflower florets and cook for 7 minutes. Drain and set aside.

Preheat the oven to 75–80°C (167–176°F/Gas ¼ or less). Bring another pan of salted water to the boil, add the cabbage leaves and cook for 1 minute. Drain and transfer briefly to a bowl of iced water to help retain the colour. Drain again, pat dry with paper towels, then brush the leaves lightly on both sides with olive oil. Arrange on a baking sheet and cover with a sheet of baking parchment (parchment paper), then place in the preheated oven and cook for 1 hour, until dry and crisp. Remove from the oven and set aside.

Meanwhile, cut the cod into cubes and the cauliflower florets into quarters. Put both in a pan and add the drained, sliced potatoes, the milk, cream and thyme. Add salt and cook over a low heat for 10–12 minutes until the fish is cooked through and the potatoes are tender. Strain through a fine sieve, reserving the liquid as well as the cod and the vegetables.

Heat half the oil in a pan over a low heat and add the drained cod and vegetables. Mix gently. Add the cooking liquid, a little at a time, and the remaining oil. Cook gently to ensure that the liquid is absorbed slowly. When the brandade is smooth and creamy, remove from the heat. Serve with the crisp cabbage leaves.

Many different cabbages

Torta di radicchio, mele secche e pistacchi al caramello
Caramel radicchio tart with dried apple and pistachios

I firmly believe that very different ingredients will only enhance one another if they are in the right proportions and their tastes mesh. The bitterness of the radicchio provides a cheerful note in this monumental dessert. The pistachios bask in the sugary flavour of the dried apple and then the teeth meet the crunchy caramel.

Serves 6

for the pastry (pie dough)
300g (10oz/2 cups) 00 flour, plus extra for dusting

1 level tbsp caster (superfine) sugar

pinch of salt

150g (5oz/scant ⅔ cup) unsalted butter, softened and diced, plus extra for greasing

2–3 tbsp iced water

for the filling
head of Treviso radicchio

100g (3½oz/½ cup) caster (superfine) sugar, plus 2 tbsp

100g (3½oz/scant ½ cup) unsalted butter, softened and diced

100g (3½oz/⅔ cup) almond flour

1 egg

30g (1oz/scant ¼ cup) pistachio nuts, shelled and coarsely chopped

100g (3½oz) dried apple rings

for the caramel
4 tbsp water

200g (7oz/scant 1 cup) caster (superfine) sugar

1 tsp lemon juice

Make the pastry (pie dough). Sift the flour into a bowl and mix with the sugar and salt. Make a well in the centre and add the butter. Rub the butter into the flour using the fingertips until it resembles crumbs. Add 1 tbsp iced water at a time and blend it in to make a smooth, soft dough. Wrap in clingfilm (plastic wrap) and refrigerate for 1 hour.

Meanwhile, prepare the filling. Preheat the oven to 180°C (350°F/Gas 4). Bring a pan of water to the boil over a high heat, reduce the heat and add the radicchio and 2 tbsp sugar. Simmer for a minute or so to soften, then drain. Carefully squeeze out the excess water, then roughly chop the radicchio and set aside. Beat the softened butter, almond flour, remaining sugar and egg together in a bowl until smooth. Add the chopped radicchio, the pistachios and half the dried apple.

Grease and flour a 24cm (9½in) diameter tart tin (pan). Roll out the pastry (pie dough) on a floured surface to a thickness of 5mm (¼in) and use to line the tin (pan). Cover the pastry (pie dough) with the remaining dried apple and pour the radicchio mixture over the top. Place in the preheated oven and cook for 35–40 minutes, until the top is golden and the inside is completely dry. Remove from the oven and leave to cool.

Meanwhile, make the caramel. Put the water and sugar in a small saucepan over a low heat until the sugar has dissolved. Add the lemon juice and continue to cook until the syrup is a light amber colour. To serve, remove the tart from the tin (pan), pour a very thin layer of caramel over and arrange on a cake stand or serving plate. Refrigerate for at least 1 hour.

Meli-melò di radicchi con salame fresco scottato e vinaigrette al sidro
Meli-melò radicchio salad with crispy salami and cider vinaigrette

This dish is fit for a king. It is true that the more varieties you use the more you will enjoy it, but it will still be sublime if you manage to find just a single good variety of fresh radicchio and an equally good fresh salami.

PICTURED ON PREVIOUS PAGE

Serves 6

1 head of Treviso radicchio

1 head of Verona radicchio

1 head of variegated Castelfranco radicchio

12 Rosa di Gorizia radicchio buds

handful of wild radicchio

200ml (7fl oz/generous ¾ cup) extra virgin olive oil

70ml (scant 3fl oz/generous ¼ cup) cider

6 slices of fresh pork salami

salt and freshly ground black pepper

Wash and dry the radicchio well. Make the vinaigrette in a bowl by whisking together the olive oil and cider. Add salt and pepper to taste.

Heat a dry non-stick frying pan for a minute or two, then add the slices of salami and fry for no more than 1 minute on each side, until golden all over. Remove with a slotted spoon and cut into small pieces.

To serve, put a mixture of radicchio leaves on each plate. Add the pieces of fried salami and dress with the vinaigrette.

Tempura di radicchio
Radicchio tempura

Thanks to its versatility, radicchio has become the basis for some unlikely combinations. This recipe is an example. It is always a success, especially when served with a bubbly aperitif.

Serves 6

3 heads of radicchio (Treviso and Verona)

peanut or rapeseed oil, for deep-frying

250g (8oz/1⅔ cups) 00 flour

500ml (17fl oz/2 cups) sparkling water, chilled

salt

Wash and dry the radicchio well. Divide into pieces lengthways. Heat the peanut or rapeseed oil in a deep pan over a medium to high heat to no more than 170°C (340°F).

Meanwhile, make the tempura batter. Put the flour in a bowl and add the sparkling water. Mix together well. Dip the radicchio pieces, 2 at a time, into the batter, making sure they are well coated.

Deep-fry the radicchio in the hot oil for 3 minutes until crispy. Remove with a slotted spoon and drain on paper towels. Sprinkle with salt and serve immediately.

Filetto di dentice golden-brown con piccola insalatina di radicchio Rosa di Gorizia con vinaigrette alla mela
Pan-fried snapper with pink Gorizia radicchio salad and apple vinaigrette

I love the definition of the small pink Gorizia radicchio as 'a product of refined culture and the farmer's sensitivity'. This explains why the families who still produce it pride themselves on growing the most beautiful and the very best radicchio. It has an intense, slightly bitter flavour and a bright red colour imbued with hues of different intensity.

Serves 6

3 tbsp extra virgin olive oil

6 red snapper fillets

for the salad

18 heads of young Rosa di Gorizia radicchio or 12 hearts of any type of radicchio

100ml (3½fl oz/scant ½ cup) extra virgin olive oil

50ml (2fl oz/scant ¼ cup) cider vinegar

1 cooking apple, peeled, cored and cut into cubes

salt and freshly ground black pepper

Make the salad by washing and drying the radicchio. Whisk the olive oil and vinegar together in a bowl to make an emulsion, add salt and pepper to taste, then stir in the cubed apple and set aside.

Heat a non-stick frying pan containing enough olive oil to cover the base over a medium heat, taking care not to burn the oil. Arrange the snapper fillets, skin side down, in the hot oil and cook for 3 minutes. Turn over and cook for no longer than 2 minutes, until the fish is cooked through.

Serve the snapper with the radicchio salad and apple vinaigrette.

Tortelli ripieni di radicchio di Treviso, radicchio variegato di Castelfranco e d'oca affumicato al burro al timo fresco
Castelfranco radicchio and smoked goose-filled tortelli with thyme-scented butter

The smoking of the goose breast is barely perceptible but gently sweetens the meat, while the thyme-scented butter adds a fresh touch. Castelfranco radicchio tastes delicate so if you can't get any, avoid using a bitter radicchio. The finished dish provides an elegant and well-balanced array of flavours.

Serves 6

for the pasta
400g (13oz/2⅔ cups) 00 flour
2 eggs
4 egg yolks
pinch of salt

for the filling
200g (7oz) Treviso radicchio
200g (7oz) variegated Castelfranco radicchio
2 shallots, peeled and finely sliced
1 tbsp extra virgin olive oil
200g (7oz) smoked goose breast, thinly sliced and cut into julienne strips
1 egg yolk
150g (5oz/scant 2¼ cups) breadcrumbs
salt and freshly ground black pepper

for the thyme-scented butter
2 small bunches of thyme, plus extra to garnish
300g (10oz/scant 1¼ cups) unsalted butter, softened

Start by making the pasta. Sift the flour onto a work surface in a mound, make a well in the centre, add the eggs, egg yolks and salt and mix thoroughly. Knead for 15 minutes, until the dough is smooth and stretchy. Work into a ball and wrap in clingfilm (plastic wrap). Leave to rest in a cool place for about 1 hour.

Meanwhile, make the filling. Wash and dry the radicchio, then cut into julienne strips. Put the shallots in a pan over a medium heat with the olive oil. As soon as the shallots are soft, add the julienned goose breast. Stir once, then add the radicchio, stirring continuously. Continue to cook until wilted. Season with a little salt to taste. Remove the pan from the heat and leave to cool, then blend lightly so the mixture retains some texture.

Add the egg yolk and breadcrumbs and mix in carefully. Set aside.

Make the thyme-scented butter. Finely chop the thyme, then add to the softened butter. Set aside.

To make the tortelli, divide the pasta into 2 balls on a floured surface and roll each out thinly to a thickness of 1–1.5mm (1/16in). Place evenly spaced walnut-sized blobs of filling on the first sheet of pasta. Cover with the second sheet, pressing the pasta down well around the filling so that all the air is squeezed out and to seal well. Cut the tortelli up using a frilled pasta wheel.

Bring a large pan of salted water to the boil over a high heat. Add the tortelli and cook for 5–6 minutes, until the tortelli float to the surface.

Meanwhile, melt the thyme-scented butter in a bain-marie.

When the tortelli are ready, scoop them out of the water with a slotted spoon and transfer to a warmed serving plate. Pour over the melted butter, then garnish with a few sprigs of thyme and a sprinkle of black pepper.

Crema di radicchio di Treviso e Verona con scampi e porri
Creamed radicchio soup with scampi and leeks

Generally, the Venetian types of radicchio are interchangeable but some are more bitter than others. Here I temper the bitterness of the Treviso radicchio by adding the Veronan variety, which is more delicate-tasting.

Serves 6

300g (10oz) Treviso radicchio

300g (10oz) Verona radicchio

1 leek

1 onion

2 small potatoes

3 tbsp extra virgin olive oil, plus extra to drizzle

1 litre (1¾ pints/4 cups) vegetable stock

50g (2oz/⅓ cup) plain (all-purpose) flour, sifted

100ml (3½fl oz/scant ½ cup) single (light) cream

18 very fresh raw scampi, in the shell

salt and freshly ground black pepper

Wash the radicchio and cut into julienne strips. Wash the leek, reserving some of the green parts for later use. Finely chop the rest of the leek. Peel and chop the onion finely, and peel and dice the potatoes.

Heat 1 tbsp of the olive oil in a pan over a low heat, add the chopped leek and onion and cook for 5–6 minutes, then add the potato. Cook for 7–8 minutes, stirring continuously.

Add 3–4 tbsp of the vegetable stock and stir. Continue to cook until the stock has almost evaporated, then add the julienne of radicchio and salt to taste. Continue stirring, add the rest of the stock and cook for 10 minutes more. Remove from the heat and whizz the mixture with a hand blender until smooth and creamy. If necessary, strain through a fine sieve. Return the soup to the heat and add the flour, stirring well to avoid lumps. Cook for 15 minutes more over a low heat, then add the cream.

Remove the heads and shells from the scampi and discard the black filaments. Cut the reserved leek into thin strips. Heat the remaining olive oil in a frying pan over a medium heat, add the leek strips and cook for 1 minute, stirring. Add the scampi tails and cook until golden, 2–3 minutes maximum, continuing to stir. Serve the radicchio soup garnished with the scampi, leek strips, a dusting of black pepper and a drizzle of olive oil.

'A smile to look at and paradise to eat ... the Treviso radicchio.'

Thus runs the official anthem of the radicchio, written by Giovanni Rizzi in 1876. Will all those who have never heard of radicchio please raise their hands. Although I would expect all hands to stay down, I am still going to talk just a little about the radicchio. I am Venetian, which means that talking about it is just too strong a temptation. Veneto is without doubt the perfect region for the cultivation of the radicchio. Indeed, the largest and best areas of production lie close to our house. There the varieties grown include the Treviso red, the Castelfranco variegated, the Chioggia red and the Verona red. Radicchio is incredibly versatile; it lends itself well to a multitude of recipes for appetizers, starters, main courses and desserts. I also find it remarkably decorative. I have often used radicchio in place of flowers to make small bouquets or centrepieces and the result has always been striking. Nowadays radicchio is well known almost everywhere and may therefore be found without difficulty at the best-stocked greengrocers.

Soufflè di radicchio di Verona, formaggio Montasio e miele di Corbezzolo
Radicchio, cheese and honey soufflés

This soufflé is a perfect lunch or dinner starter. Don't be tempted to open the oven door before time or you may find yourself picking up the pieces of your failed venture. And serve immediately, as soufflés have a tendency to sink very quickly even when perfectly executed.

Serves 6

400g (13oz) Verona radicchio

60g (2½oz/¼ cup) unsalted butter, plus extra for greasing

4 tbsp plain (all-purpose) flour, sifted

750ml (1¼ pints/3 cups) full-cream (whole) milk

4 eggs, separated

50g (2oz) Montasio cheese, or any other fresh cow's milk cheese with a little seasoning, grated

2 tsp Corbezzolo or chestnut honey

2 tbsp dry breadcrumbs

salt and freshly ground black pepper

Preheat the oven to 200°C (400°F/Gas 6). Wash the radicchio and cut into julienne strips. Bring a pan of salted water to the boil over a high heat. Add the prepared radicchio, reduce the heat and cook for 2 minutes. Drain and squeeze out any excess water.

Melt the butter in a clean saucepan, then add the flour, stirring well with a wooden spoon to avoid lumps. When the mixture is smooth, add the milk and mix well until the sauce starts to thicken. Remove from the heat and add the radicchio, egg yolks, grated cheese and honey. Add salt and pepper to taste and leave to cool.

Butter 6 individual soufflé moulds and sprinkle with the breadcrumbs, then discard any excess. Whisk the egg whites in a bowl until stiff and dry, then fold into the cooled radicchio mixture, a little at a time. Pour the mixture into the prepared moulds, place in the preheated oven and cook for 15 minutes until golden brown and risen, taking care not to open the oven during this time. Serve immediately.

Radicchio

Dacquise di mandorle con mousse al pistacchio e mela morbida
Almond dacquoise with pistachio mousse and apple

This recipe offers a splendid, exquisitely balanced contrast between the almond dacquoise and the pistachio mousse that is further enhanced by the exceptionally delicate, slightly tangy taste of the pieces of apple. It makes a happy ending for happy tables.

Serves 6

for the dacquoise

60g (2½oz/scant ½ cup) 00 flour

170g (scant 6oz/generous 1⅓ cups) ground almonds

300g (10oz/generous 1⅓ cups) caster (superfine) sugar

8 egg whites

for the mousse

400g (13oz) white chocolate

120g (scant 4oz/generous ¾ cup) pistachio nuts, shelled and peeled, plus extra to serve

knob of unsalted butter

1 tsp leaf gelatine

200ml (7fl oz/generous ¾ cup) full-cream (whole) milk

4 egg yolks

3 egg whites

60g (2½oz/generous ¼ cup) caster (superfine) sugar

for the apple

3 cooking apples

2 tbsp unrefined cane sugar

a few drops of lemon juice

Make the dacquoise. Preheat the oven to 200°C (400°F/Gas 6). Sift the flour with the ground almonds and 200g (7oz/scant 1 cup) of the sugar. Set aside. Whisk the egg whites with the remaining sugar. When the whites are stiff, gently fold in the flour and almond mixture a little at a time. Line a baking sheet with baking parchment (parchment paper) and arrange 6 tian rings or moulds 9cm (3½in) in diameter on the parchment. Transfer the dacquoise mixture to a piping (pastry) bag and pipe a little of the mixture at a time into the tian rings until they are one-third full. Place in the preheated oven and cook for 15 minutes or until just golden. Remove from the oven and leave to cool.

Meanwhile, make the mousse. Cut the chocolate into small pieces and set aside. Grind the pistachio nuts to a fine powder. Put the nuts in a heavy-based pan with the butter and cook over a low heat for 10 minutes, stirring continuously, until they form a paste. Soak the gelatine in cold water for 10 minutes, then squeeze it out well.

Meanwhile, put the milk in a pan and bring to the boil over a medium heat, then remove from the heat and add the squeezed-out gelatine. Stir well until the gelatine has completely dissolved, then add the pieces of chocolate followed by the pistachio mixture and the egg yolks. Mix everything together until smooth.

Put the egg whites and sugar in a clean bowl, whisk together until stiff and fold into the chocolate and pistachio mixture. Divide between the tian rings, pouring it on top of the dacquoises to fill the rings. Freeze for 3 hours.

Meanwhile, prepare the apple. Peel the apples, cut into small pieces and discard the cores. Put the apple into a non-stick pan with the sugar and lemon juice and cook over a low heat for 5 minutes, or until the apple has begun to soften but still has some bite.

When the mousse in the tian rings has set, remove from the freezer. Release the dacquoises from the tian rings, using the point of a knife dipped in hot water. To serve, arrange on plates and decorate with a little of the apple mixture and a few pistachio nuts.

Torta al prosecco con sciroppo al vino moscato
Prosecco torta with moscato syrup

This torta is relatively easy to make and has a truly delicate flavour. I have fun using a slightly retro-looking cake tin (pan), but you can use any suitably sized tin (pan). The torta is ideally served at the end of dinner, after the main dessert, as a sweet accompaniment to never-ending evenings.

Serves 6–8

unsalted butter, for greasing

100g (3½oz/⅔ cup) plain (all-purpose) flour, sifted, plus extra for dusting

5 egg yolks

100g (3½oz/½ cup) caster (superfine) sugar

75ml (3fl oz/scant ⅓ cup) extra virgin olive oil

150ml (¼ pint/scant ⅔ cup) Prosecco

pinch of saffron threads, soaked in 80ml (3fl oz/ ⅓ cup) warm water

pinch of salt

7 egg whites

pinch of cream of tartar

icing (confectioners') sugar, for dusting

for the Moscato syrup

250ml (8fl oz/1 cup) water

250ml (8fl oz/1 cup) Moscato or other dessert wine

250g (8oz/generous 1 cup) caster (superfine) sugar

pinch of saffron powder

Preheat the oven to 180°C (350°F/Gas 4). Grease and flour a 20cm (8in) diameter cake tin (pan). Put the egg yolks in a bowl with half of the sugar and beat until thick, creamy and pale. Add the olive oil, Prosecco and the saffron infusion. Add the sifted flour and salt and mix well. Set aside.

Put the egg whites, remaining sugar and cream of tartar in another bowl and whisk until the mixture is stiff but not dry. Add the egg yolk mixture and fold in.

Pour the mixture into a 20cm (8in) cake tin (pan), place in the preheated oven and cook for 20 minutes, then reduce the temperature to 150°C (300°F/Gas 2) and cook for 20 minutes more. Turn off the oven, cover the cake with a sheet of baking parchment (parchment paper) and leave in the turned-off oven for 10 minutes more.

Meanwhile, make the Moscato syrup. Put the water, Moscato and sugar in a heavy-based pan, bring to the boil over a high heat, then add the saffron powder. Reduce the heat to medium and continue to cook until the Moscato has reduced to a thick syrup. Remove from the heat and leave to cool.

When the torta is ready, remove from the oven and turn it out of the tin (pan), Dust with icing (confectioners') sugar and serve sliced, with the Moscato syrup.

San Pietro agli agrumi
Citrus-scented fillet of John Dory

John Dory is high on the list of the fish I most like to serve. Here I prepare it whole, cooked in the oven, with all the flavour and colours of southern, sun-ripened citrus fruit. Although winter lies in wait outside, the warm colours of the sun gladden our plates and hearts. PICTURED ON PREVIOUS PAGE

Serves 6–8

2 unwaxed oranges

1 unwaxed lemon

4 tbsp olive oil

1 tbsp small salted capers

2 garlic cloves

2 John Dory (or swordfish, sea bream, sea bass or snapper), about 1kg (2lb) each, cleaned and gutted

1 tsp coriander seeds

salt and freshly ground white pepper

Preheat the oven to 180°C (350°F/Gas 4). Wash the oranges and lemon and dry with paper towels. Peel the zest thinly, chop finely and set aside. Squeeze the juice of the oranges, whisk together in a bowl with the olive oil, add salt and pepper to taste, then set aside. Rinse the capers under running water to remove the salt, dry with paper towels, then set aside. Peel the garlic, cut in half and set aside. Lightly crush the coriander seeds in a pestle and mortar and set aside.

Line a large roasting tin (pan) with baking parchment (parchment paper), leaving plenty of overhang. Check that the fish have been properly cleaned and gutted, dry them with paper towels, then brush with the orange juice and oil mixture. Arrange in the lined roasting tin (pan). Sprinkle with the citrus zest, capers, garlic halves and coriander seeds. Cover with another sheet of baking parchment (parchment paper) the same size as the first and fold over the edges of the parchment to create a parcel with the fish inside.

Place in the preheated oven and cook for 25 minutes, but check how the fish is doing after 15 minutes. The fish is ready when the flesh looks white, feels firm and comes away from the bone easily without losing its shape. Remove the fish from the oven. To serve, fillet if desired and pour the pan juices on top.

Alzavole con pere e purè di finocchi
Teals with pears and fennel purée

Always choose small, preferably female teals. Their buttery flavour is in part due to their high fat content, which is balanced by the delicate, tasty meat. Here I add a fennel purée for a pleasantly fresh note. This recipe is to be recommended if you want an impressive, main meat course.

Serves 6

6 oven-ready teals

4 small pears

1 knob of unsalted butter

2 tbsp extra virgin olive oil

4 star anise

3 fresh bay leaves

3 tbsp honey

2 tbsp honey vinegar

salt and freshly ground black pepper

for the fennel purée

4 large fennel

4 tbsp extra virgin olive oil

1 garlic clove, peeled

small piece of lemon zest

450g (scant 15oz/2½ cups) cooked cannellini beans, or similar beans

Start by preparing the fennel purée. Trim the fennel and cut into small dice. Heat the olive oil in a heavy-based pan over a medium heat, add the garlic clove and prepared fennel, reduce the heat and cook over a low heat for 20 minutes, or until the fennel is soft. Add the lemon zest, cannellini beans and salt and pepper to taste, and cook for 10 minutes more, stirring continuously, until the mixture becomes smooth and creamy.

To prepare the teal, preheat the oven to 200°C (400°F/Gas 6). Wash the teal and dry thoroughly with paper towels. Wash and dry the pears, cut in half but do not remove the cores, then set aside.

Heat the butter, olive oil, star anise and bay leaves in a large frying pan over a medium heat and cook gently until the butter has melted. Add the teal and cook for 2 minutes on each side to brown all over, then add the halved pears and cook for 4 minutes.

Add the honey to the pan and continue to cook until it caramelizes, then add the vinegar and continue to cook until this has evaporated. Add salt and pepper to taste and continue to cook for 5 minutes more, turning the teal in the caramel for the flavours to develop.

Remove the pan from the heat and transfer the teal and the pears to a roasting dish. Pour the pan juices on top. Place in the preheated oven and cook for 15 minutes. Remove from the oven and test for doneness; the meat should be moist and still a little pink. Cut the teal in half and serve each portion with half a pear and some fennel purée.

Risotto con cardo selvatico e erbe
Risotto of wild cardoons and herbs

Cardoons are close relatives of artichokes and have a very similar taste, only slightly sweeter. Choose fleshy but firm cardoons with a good ivory colour and remove the tougher, outer ribs. Once cut, like artichokes, cardoons should be dipped in acidulated water to prevent them from turning unappealingly black.

Serves 6

4 wild cardoons

3 tbsp extra virgin olive oil

2 shallots, finely chopped

a few rosemary, oregano and mint leaves, finely chopped

1 litre (1¾ pints/4 cups) (about) vegetable stock

450g (scant 15oz/2¼ cups) Vialone Nano or Carnaroli rice

60g (2½oz/¾ cup) grated Parmesan cheese (or half Parmesan cheese and half Pecorino cheese)

salt and freshly ground black pepper

Clean the cardoons, discard any stringy bits, then cut into dice. Heat the olive oil in a pan over a medium heat, add the shallots and cook for 4 minutes, then add the prepared cardoons and the chopped herbs. Sauté for 10 minutes, then add salt to taste (taking into account the saltiness of the stock), and continue to cook for 1–2 minutes, stirring occasionally while the flavours develop.

Bring the stock to the boil in a saucepan over a high heat, reduce the heat and leave to simmer. Meanwhile, add the rice to the pan with the cardoons and cook for 2 minutes, stirring continuously.

Add the boiling stock to the rice, a ladleful at a time, stirring continuously and waiting until each ladleful has almost been absorbed before adding the next. Continue adding stock until the rice is ready – al dente but still moist. Remove the pan from the heat and stir in the cheese. Serve immediately.

Gran crema di canocchie
Cream of mantis prawn soup

This haute cuisine dish has a delicate, intense and extremely well-balanced flavour. Mantis prawns are generally easy to find, although of course they should be extremely fresh, if not actually live. Just give your regular fishmonger a few days' warning, then relish the applause when you serve the dish to family and friends.

Serves 6

2 onions

sprig of parsley

1 carrot

4 white peppercorns

pinch of coarse sea salt

24 mantis prawns (shrimp)

2 garlic cloves

4 tbsp extra virgin olive oil

40–50ml (2fl oz/scant ¼ cup) dry white wine

4 salted anchovy fillets, rinsed

250ml (8fl oz/1 cup) single (light) cream

freshly ground white pepper

1 tbsp cornflour (cornstarch), dissolved in 4 tbsp milk

for the croûtons

6 slices of bread

knob of unsalted butter

Cut 1 onion in half and put in a large saucepan with the parsley, carrot, peppercorns and sea salt. Cover with plenty of water, bring to the boil over a high heat and cook for 5 minutes. Meanwhile, wash the prawns (shrimp) in cold running water. Add to the pan of boiling stock and cook for 20 minutes more.

Strain the stock through a fine sieve, discard any remaining prawn (shrimp), then return the stock to the pan. Bring to the boil again, then continue to cook to reduce it to about 1 litre (1¾ pints/4 cups).

Meanwhile, peel and finely chop the other onion and the garlic, put in a pan with the olive oil and cook over a medium heat for 5 minutes, until transparent. Add the wine and continue to cook for 4–5 minutes, or until the wine has evaporated.

Chop the anchovy fillets very finely and add to the pan with the reduced stock. Reduce the heat and simmer for 15 minutes. Add the cream and the white pepper, stir well, then strain through a fine sieve. Return to the pan, bring back to the boil, then add the cornflour (cornstarch) dissolved in the milk. Cook for 7 minutes more, until the soup has thickened.

Meanwhile, make the croûtons. Cut the crusts off the bread, cut into small cubes and put in a frying pan with the butter over a medium heat. Fry until golden brown.

Serve the soup garnished with the croûtons and a dusting of freshly ground white pepper.

Comfortable and welcoming. These two words embrace my way of receiving guests and even of looking on life. Every time we organize something at home, whether for close or more 'formal' friends, I always want to welcome them into a cosy, calm atmosphere. When decorating the house, planning its different spaces and deciding on their use, I am largely guided by these concepts, which I find instinctive rather than rational. Partying with friends is for me, first of all, the light of thousands of candles; they warm the heart and lift the spirits so as to make people favourably inclined towards others. The organization as a whole should be impeccable, although by this I don't mean to suggest that I have put my name down for the 'best hostess of the year' competition. I just want to stress that an invitation is a gift we offer people who are important to us and, as such, it should be well thought out and thoroughly prepared. Our gift will therefore be a correctly and elegantly laid table, without pomp, and a buffet that is rich in tasty, well-presented dishes – dishes that are even tailored to the tastes of our dearest friends. With this I am satisfied.

Insalata di carciofi crudi con noci e panna chantilly all'aglio
Artichoke and walnut salad with garlic chantilly cream

This refined little salad is at its best when the artichokes are young and extremely fresh. They should have tight leaves, be very pale in colour and have an unmistakable, sweetly aromatic note. The garlic Chantilly is perfect with the creamy, delicate taste of the walnuts and the hint of bitterness of the artichokes.

Serves 6

5 garlic cloves

500ml (17fl oz/2 cups) whipping cream

6 artichokes

juice of 1 lemon

18 walnuts, in their shells

2 tbsp light extra virgin olive oil

salt and freshly ground black pepper

Peel the garlic and cut in half lengthways, discarding any central green shoots. Put in a pan over a low heat with the cream and cook, stirring occasionally, for 10 minutes. Add salt and pepper to taste, then transfer to a blender and whizz until smooth. Strain through a fine sieve and pour into a cream siphon. Pressurize with 1 or 2 cream chargers depending on the size of the siphon (use 1 for a 500ml/17fl oz siphon, 2 for a 1,000ml/1¾ pint siphon). Shake the siphon and leave in the refrigerator for at least 3 hours before using.

Prepare the artichokes. Carefully remove the tough outer leaves, trim off the tough tips of the remaining leaves, remove the choke and trim the stem down to its tender part. Cut the artichokes in half, then slice thinly widthways. Add the lemon juice to a large bowl of water, then immerse the sliced artichokes in the acidulated water for 10 minutes. This will stop them discolouring.

Remove the artichokes from the water and pat dry with paper towels. Crack open the walnuts, place in a bowl and add the dried artichokes. Add salt and pepper and the olive oil, then mix well.

To serve, remove the siphon from the refrigerator, give it a good shake and squeeze out a bed of garlic Chantilly cream onto each serving plate. Arrange a serving of the artichoke and walnut salad on top.

Cosy celebration with friends

WINTER

Marmellata di pere con noci di macadamia, sauternes e rosmarino
Pear jam with macadamia, walnut, sauternes and rosemary

This unusual jam is the perfect balance of ingredients; the sweet, buttery macadamia nut goes well with the cool flesh of the pear, and the honey notes of the Sauternes bind the flavours together perfectly. The final touch of rosemary gives further cohesion and lightness to the taste. *Molto andante.*

Yield: 1 litre (1¾ pints/4 cups)

1.5kg (3lb) Williams pears, peeled, cored and cut into medium-sized pieces

900g (1¾lb/4 cups) granulated sugar

100ml (3½fl oz/scant ½ cup) Sauternes

sprig of rosemary

70g (scant 3oz/½ cup) macadamia nuts

Put the pieces of pear in a spacious flameproof pan over a medium heat, add the sugar and leave to cook for around 15 minutes.

Add the Sauternes and the sprig of rosemary. Continue to cook for 20 minutes more.

When the pears have softened and you have a smooth mixture, add the macadamia nuts.

Check for set by putting a teaspoonful on a cold plate (see p.83), then pour into jars. Eat straight away or sterilize (see p.148) and keep for up to 6 months.

This is good with most types of cheese; try Fossa, Pecorino toscano, Gorgonzola, Asiago, Tete de Moine and Roquefort.

Mostarda di frutta mista alla cremonese
Mixed spicy fruit 'mustard' alla cremonese

Northern Italy is the home of this fruit-based preserve that was born out of the need to preserve anything that could not be used fresh. Today, because of its wonderful sweet spicy taste, fruit mustard is served with game, mixed boiled meats – *bollito misto* (see p.129) – and also cheeses and cured meats. *Andante con moto.*
PICTURED ON PAGE 131

Serves 6–8

2kg (4lb) mixed fruit (such as peaches, apricots, small pears, cherries,mandarins, figs)

1kg (2lb/4½ cups) granulated sugar

1 litre (1¾ pints/4 cups) water

10 drops of mustard essence

Wash and thoroughly dry the fruit. Halve the peaches and apricots and remove the stones (pits). Peel the pears, cut in half and remove the cores. Stone (pit) the cherries. Cut the mandarins in half but do not peel. Leave the figs whole.

Pour the sugar into a heavy-based pan, add the water and bring to the boil over a high heat, stirring frequently to dissolve the sugar. Reduce the heat and simmer for 20 minutes. Remove from the heat and leave to cool, then add the mustard essence and stir for 1–2 minutes. Return the pan to a medium heat and add the fruit, the bigger pieces first. Cover the pan, reduce the heat to very low and cook for 2 hours, until the fruit is cooked but still firm. Using a slotted spoon, transfer the fruit to a large jar, pour the syrup over the top and seal. Keep in a cool, dark place until required.

Marmellata d'uva bianca al profumo di thé verde alla mandorla
Grape jam scented with green almond tea

Use a green almond tea or any aromatic tea, but not fruit tea as this can either be too subtle or too heavily scented. I use small, very sweet wine-making grapes as they make a really good sweet jam. *Adagio maestoso.*

Yield: 1 litre (1¾ pints/4 cups)

2kg (4lb) green grapes

800g (1½lb/scant 3⅔ cups) granulated sugar, plus extra for the tea

100ml (3½fl oz/scant ½ cup) prepared green almond tea

Wash the grapes, separate them and put into a large heavy-based pan. Crush them lightly, then add the sugar. Leave to macerate for 2 hours, then put the pan over a high heat and cook for 20 minutes.

Add a little sugar to the tea, then add this to the grapes. Cook for 30 minutes more, simmering over a low heat. Check for set by putting a teaspoonful on a cold plate (see p.83), then pour into jars while the jam is still hot. Eat straight away or sterilize (see p.148) and keep for up to 6 months.

Goes well with...

Scones Scones

Yield: 12 scones

450g (scant 15oz/3 cups) self-raising (self-rising) flour or 450g (scant 15oz/3 cups) 00 flour plus 2 tsp baking powder, plus extra for dusting

1 tsp salt

55g (2oz/¼ cup) unsalted butter, diced

1 tbsp lemon juice

400ml (14fl oz/1¾ cups) full-cream (whole) milk, plus extra for brushing

Preheat the oven to 230°C (450°F/Gas 8) and line a baking sheet with baking parchment (parchment paper). Sift the flour, salt and baking powder, if using, into a large bowl and add the butter. Rub the butter into the flour using the fingertips until it resembles crumbs.

Whisk the lemon juice and milk together in another bowl for 1 minute, then work this mixture quickly into the crumb mixture. The wetter the dough, the lighter the scones will be.

Roll out the dough on a floured surface to a thickness of 2.5cm (1in), then, using a 5cm (2in) round cutter, cut out 12 circles of dough. Transfer to the baking sheet and brush with milk. Place in the preheated oven and cook for 20 minutes, until golden brown. Serve warm.

Marmalade teabread Marmalade teabread

Yield: 10–12 slices

200g (7oz/1⅓ cups) 00 flour

1 tsp baking powder

1 tsp ground cinnamon

100g (3½oz/scant ½ cup) unsalted butter, diced

55g (2oz/¼ cup) caster (superfine) sugar

1 egg

60ml (2½fl oz/¼ cup) orange marmalade

45ml (2fl oz/scant ¼ cup) full-cream (whole) milk

to decorate

60ml (2½fl oz) prepared glacé icing (frosting)

zest of 1 orange, grated

Preheat the oven to 160°C (325°F/Gas 3) and line a 26 x 10cm (10 x 4in) cake tin (pan) with baking parchment (parchment paper). Sift the flour with the baking powder and cinnamon into a large bowl, then add the diced butter. Rub the butter into the dry ingredients using the fingertips until it resembles crumbs. Stir in the sugar.

In another bowl, beat the egg with the marmalade and most of the milk, then add this to the crumb mixture, adding extra milk if necessary. The mixture should be soft and fairly liquid.

Transfer the mixture to the cake tin (pan), then place in the preheated oven and cook for about 1¼ hours, until firm and cooked inside. Remove from the oven and leave to cool for 5 minutes, then transfer to a wire cooling rack and remove the baking parchment (parchment paper). Leave to cool completely, then pour the glacé icing (frosting) on top and when it has set, decorate with the orange zest.

Marmellata di cachi alle fave di tonka e cognac
Persimmon jam with tonka beans and cognac

This is the *sinfonia in crescendo*. The sweet quasi-astringency of the ripe persimmons, enhanced by the hints of honey and vanilla of the tonka beans, form a prelude to the warm flavours of the cocoa. If you cannot get tonka beans, use a Madagascan vanilla pod (bean) instead. *Allegro vivace assai.*

Yield: 1 litre (1¾ pints/4 cups)

2kg (4lb) ripe persimmons
700g (scant 1½lb/scant 3¼ cups) granulated sugar
3 tonka beans, finely grated
3 generous tbsp cognac

Wash and slice the persimmons, then put through a food mill. Place in a saucepan and add the sugar and grated tonka beans. Bring to the boil over a medium heat, then add the cognac, reduce the heat and cook for 30 minutes more, until the jam is soft, but not too thick. Check for set by putting a teaspoonful on a cold plate (see p.83), then pour into jars.

Eat straight away or sterilize (see p.148) and keep for 6–8 months.

Goes well with...

Tortino colante al cioccolato caldo
Muffins dripping with melted chocolate

Serves 6

250g (8oz) plain (semisweet) chocolate (70%)
270g (9oz/generous 1 cup) unsalted butter
9 eggs
400g (13oz/generous 1¾ cups) caster (superfine) sugar
125g (4oz/generous ¾ cup) plain (all-purpose) flour, sifted

Preheat the oven to 210°C (410°F/Gas 6½). Place the chocolate and butter in a bain-marie and melt over a low heat. Gently mix the eggs with the sugar and warm in another bain-marie.

Add the flour to the chocolate and butter mixture, mix well, then add the warmed egg and sugar mixture and mix well again.

Pour into a 6-hole non-stick muffin pan (tin), place in the preheated oven and bake for 8 minutes, until the muffins have risen but are still creamy inside.

Composta di zucca in agrodolce
Sweet and sour pumpkin preserve

This preserve makes a perfect accompaniment to the classic veal tagine (see below). This kind of dish has become a well accepted part of our culinary culture. I like to serve it from a big platter in the centre of the table; it makes an aromatic one-dish meal. *Allegretto vivace.* PICTURED ON PAGE 151

Yield: 1 litre (1¾ pints/4 cups)

50ml (2fl oz/scant ¼ cup) extra virgin olive oil

2 onions, peeled and finely chopped

1kg (2lb) pumpkin, peeled, deseeded and cut into chunks

50ml (2fl oz/scant ¼ cup) white wine

2 tsp curry powder

salt

8–10 black peppercorns

1 small cinnamon stick

Heat the olive oil in a pan over a medium heat, add the onions and cook for 3–4 minutes, until soft. Add the pumpkin, wine and curry powder and stir well. Add salt to taste, the peppercorns and cinnamon stick.

Reduce the heat to low and continue to cook for 25 minutes, or until the pumpkin is soft and the mixture is smooth.

Transfer the pumpkin to jars. Eat straight away or sterilize (see p.148) and keep for up to 6 months.

Goes well with...
Tajine di vitello Veal tagine

Serves 6

3 tbsp extra virgin olive oil

3 small onions, peeled and finely chopped

4 carrots, peeled and halved

200g (7oz/1 cup) chickpeas, soaked overnight in cold water, then drained

1.5kg (3lb) stewing veal, cut into pieces

3 slices of unwaxed lemon

1 tsp cumin powder

pinch of saffron threads

4 courgettes (zucchini), sliced

3 small tomatoes, chopped and deseeded

½ small pumpkin, peeled, deseeded and roughly chopped

100g (3½oz/generous ½ cup) raisins, soaked for 20 minutes in cold water, then drained

2 sprigs of coriander (cilantro), finely chopped

1 onion, peeled and finely sliced, to garnish

salt and freshly ground black pepper

Heat the olive oil in a pan over a medium heat, add the onions and cook for 3–4 minutes until soft. Reduce the heat and add the carrots, chickpeas, veal, lemon slices, cumin, saffron and salt and pepper. Cook for 25 minutes.

Add the courgettes (zucchini), tomatoes, pumpkin and soaked raisins. Cook for 20 minutes more, then add the chopped coriander (cilantro). Serve garnished with slices of raw onion.

Chutney di nespole e mango
Mango and medlar chutney

Variations on a classical mango chutney! The success of this recipe is in using fewer mangos and more medlars. The medlars should be picked after the first frost, when the flesh is very sweet and tastes like baked apple. *Adagio ma non troppo.* PICTURED ON PAGE 150

Yield: 500ml (17fl oz/2cups)

1 mango

500g (1lb) medlars

100g (3½oz/½ cup) granulated sugar

5 cardamom seeds

1 dried red chilli pepper

1 tsp turmeric powder

1 tsp cumin powder

1 tbsp root ginger, peeled and finely sliced

½ cinnamon stick

1 shallot, finely chopped

100ml (3½fl oz/scant ½ cup) white wine vinegar

2 tbsp raisins, soaked for 20 minutes in cold water, then drained

Peel and chop the mango into medium-sized pieces. Wash and dry the medlars. Put in a bowl with the prepared mango, cover with sugar and leave to stand for 1 hour.

Meanwhile, grind the cardamom seeds and finely chop, then crush the chilli pepper. Transfer the mango, medlars, sugar and any juice that has come from the fruit to a saucepan. Add the cardamom, turmeric, cumin, chilli, ginger, cinnamon stick and chopped shallot. Add the vinegar, stir well and bring to the boil over a high heat. Reduce the heat to its lowest setting, add the softened raisins and cook for 40 minutes more, until the liquid looks syrupy. Make sure that the liquid does not evaporate completely. Remove from the heat and pour into the jars. Eat straight away or sterilize (see p.148) and keep for up to 6 months.

Goes well with...

Riso pilaf all'indiana Indian pilaf rice

Serves 6

1 onion, peeled and finely sliced

90g (3½oz/generous ⅓ cup) unsalted butter

420g (14oz/generous 2 cups) Basmati rice

salt, to taste

Preheat the oven to 200°C (400°F/Gas 6). Put the onion and butter in a high-sided ovenproof pan over a low heat and cook until the onion is transparent, stirring frequently to ensure it does not burn.

Add the rice and continue to cook, stirring frequently, until the rice turns golden brown. Add salt to taste and enough boiling water to cover the rice one and half times. Cover with baking parchment (parchment paper) and a lid, then place in the preheated oven and cook for 16–18 minutes, or until al dente.

Serve topped with the mango and medlar chutney.

Goes well with... *Spuma di foie gras* Foie gras mousse

Serves 6

150g (5oz) duck livers
½ tsp ground cinnamon
½ tsp ground cloves
½ tsp ground nutmeg
250ml (8fl oz/1 cup) single (light) cream
freshly ground black pepper

Clean the duck livers. Place in a blender with the spices and pepper, then whizz for just a couple of seconds until the mixture is creamy. Stir in the cream and pass through a fine sieve, then pour into a cream siphon. Pressurize with 1 or 2 cream chargers depending on the size of the siphon (use 1 for a 500ml/17fl oz siphon, 2 for a 1,000ml/1¾ pint siphon). Shake the siphon and leave in the refrigerator until needed. To serve, spoon the quince and voatsiperifery jelly into individual serving glasses and squeeze the foie gras mousse on top from the cream siphon.

'A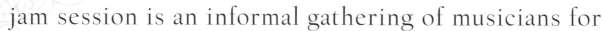 jam session is an informal gathering of musicians for the purpose of playing music without predefined arrangement through improvisation which may be based on existing forms.' This eloquent definition is equally applicable to my own jam-making sessions; I am the musician, the improvisation lies in the unusual flavours and aromas, and the existing forms of the music are all the other, more typical ingredients that are needed to make jam. The result of this 'informal gathering' is a subtle combination of strong flavours that might seem discordant, yet that ultimately work together perfectly in tempo, balance and pitch. The following exercise is both pleasant and rewarding. I sought to combine rather unusual jams with other recipes so that the qualities of each might enhance the other to obtain the desired result. They are all to be tried and enjoyed, but I have a personal weakness for the pear jam with macadamia, walnut, Sauternes and rosemary, as well as for the persimmon jam with tonka beans and cognac. And why not try the quince jelly with voatsiperifery pepper...?

Gelatina di Mele Cotogne al Voatsiperifery
Quince jelly scented with voatsiperifery pepper

Voatsiperifery pepper is the fruit of the Tsiperifery, a tropical plant found in south-eastern Madagascar. It is extremely fragrant and mildly spicy, with fruit and floral notes. *Andante con espressione.*

Yield: 1 litre (1¾ pints/4 cups)

2kg (4lb) quinces

700g (scant 1½lb/scant 3¼ cups) granulated sugar

juice of 1 lemon

½ tbsp voatsiperifery pepper or Indian Tellicherry pepper

The day before, wash the quinces and remove the down from the skin. Cut into quarters, remove the cores and put in a saucepan with just enough water to cover. Bring to the boil over a high heat, reduce the heat and simmer for 1 hour. Remove from the heat.

Line a colander with muslin or cheesecloth and set over a large bowl. Pour the quinces and their water into the lined colander and leave to drain overnight. Do not press.

The following day, transfer 1 litre (1¾ pints/4 cups) of the quince juice to a saucepan, add the sugar, lemon juice and pepper. Stir to dissolve the sugar, then bring to the boil over a low heat. Reduce the heat and cook, stirring frequently until the jelly has taken on a lovely red colour and starts to coat the back of the spoon. Check for set by putting a teaspoonful on a cold plate (see p.83), then pour into jars. Eat straight away or sterilize (see below) and keep for up to 6 months.

For best results when sterilizing, choose jars with a safety lid. Tightly close the jars and transfer to a deep pan. Add enough cold water to cover. Bring to the boil and keep at a boil for at least 1 hour, then turn off the heat and leave the jars to cool down slowly in the pan of water. When cool, remove the jars from the water and check that the centres of the lids have become concave. This is a sign that the sterilization process has been carried out correctly.

Jam session

Cannoli con gelatina di melograno
Cannoli with pomegranate jelly

This is my own special take on the renowned Sicilian *cannoli*. All I have done is replace the candied pumpkin of the original with plain chocolate and coated the exposed ends of the *cannoli* with pomegranate seeds rather than the usual candied cherry and cube of candied orange.

Serves 8

400g (13oz/2²⁄₃ cups) 00 flour

3 tbsp caster (superfine) sugar

1 tbsp unsweetened cocoa powder

pinch of salt

75g (3oz/scant ⅓ cup) lard, chilled and diced

2 eggs

4 tbsp dry Marsala wine

4 tbsp white wine vinegar

1 egg white, lightly beaten

extra virgin olive oil, for greasing and deep-frying

200g (7oz/scant 1²⁄₃ cups) pomegranate seeds, to decorate

for the filling

1 kg (2lb) very fresh sheep's ricotta cheese

600g (1¼lb/2¾ cups) caster (superfine) sugar

1 vanilla pod (bean)

150g (5oz/generous ¾ cup) plain (bittersweet) chocolate drops, chopped

for the jelly (jello)

750ml (1¼ pints/3 cups) unsweetened pomegranate juice

400g (13oz/generous 1¾ cups) caster (superfine) sugar

1 vanilla pod (bean), halved

25g (1oz) leaf gelatine

Mix the flour with the sugar, cocoa and salt. Add the lard and blend well. Add the eggs, mix well, then add the Marsala and vinegar. Work the pastry (pie dough) into a ball, wrap in clingfilm (plastic wrap), then refrigerate for 1 hour.

Roll out the pastry (pie dough) on a lightly floured surface to a thickness of 3mm (⅛in). Cut out as many 10cm (4in) diameter circles as the pastry (pie dough) allows.

Oil 8 metal cream horn moulds and wrap a circle of pastry (pie dough) round each. Stick the overlapping edges of the pastry (pie dough) together with a little beaten egg white.

Half-fill a deep pan with the olive oil and heat to no more than 170°C (340°F) over a medium heat, then add the *cannoli* and deep-fry until golden all over. Remove with a slotted spoon, drain on paper towels and leave to cool, then carefully remove the *cannoli* from the moulds.

Meanwhile, make the filling. Mix the ricotta and sugar together in a bowl and leave to rest for 10 minutes. Cut the vanilla pod (bean) in half with a sharp knife and scrape out the seeds. Add the seeds and chopped chocolate to the ricotta mixture and set aside.

To make the jelly (jello), put the pomegranate juice, sugar and halved vanilla pod (bean) in a pan over a medium heat. Bring to the boil, then reduce the heat and simmer for 10 minutes. Remove from the heat and discard the vanilla pod (bean). Leave to cool slightly.

Soak the gelatine in a little cold water, then squeeze it dry. Add to the pomegranate juice mixture, then pour into a serving dish or into individual sundae dishes.

Fill the *cannoli* with the ricotta mixture, decorate with pomegranate seeds and serve with the pomegranate jelly (jello) topped with more pomegranate seeds.

Crème brûlée all'Armagnac con croccante di mandorle e melograno
Armagnac crème brûlée with almond and pomegranate cracknel

When it comes to pudding, crème brûlée any-which-way, is my only weakness. This version, with Armagnac and a topping of crunchy almond and pomegranate seeds, is no exception. Make plenty of it and if, by chance, there is any left over, cover it with clingfilm (plastic wrap) and enjoy it for a few days more.

Serves 6–8

1 litre (1¾ pints/4 cups) single (light) cream

100g (3½oz/½ cup) caster (superfine) sugar

8 egg yolks

1 egg

2 tbsp Armagnac

for the cracknel

200g (7oz/1¼ cups) almonds, blanched and peeled

250g (8oz/generous 1 cup) caster (superfine) sugar

70g (scant 3oz/generous ½ cup) pomegranate seeds

Preheat the oven to 140°C (275°F/Gas 1). Put the cream and sugar in a pan over a medium heat and bring almost to the boil. Remove from the heat, leave to cool, then add the egg yolks and the egg. Mix thoroughly. Strain the mixture through a sieve, then add the Armagnac.

Pour the mixture into 6 ovenproof ramekins and set the ramekins in a large lidded ovenproof casserole dish. Pour boiling water into the dish so the water comes halfway up the sides of the ramekins. Cover with the lid, place in the preheated oven and cook for 40–50 minutes, until firm to the touch. Leave to cool.

Meanwhile, make the cracknel. Heat a dry frying pan over a medium heat, add the almonds and toast lightly. Leave to cool, then chop roughly and tip onto a marble slab.

Put the sugar into a saucepan over a low heat and cook for 10–15 minutes, until the sugar has melted and turned golden in colour. Watch it to make sure it does not burn. Pour the melted sugar over the almonds on the marble slab and smooth quickly with a spatula. Leave to cool, then loosen the almond cracknel from the slab, transfer to a food processor and whizz to reduce the cracknel to crumbs.

To serve, mix the cracknel crumbs with the pomegranate seeds and sprinkle over the top of the crèmes brûlées.

Succo di melograno
Pomegranate juice

All that is needed to make this recipe is patience. The results are a surprise – freshly squeezed pomegranate juice is refreshing, smooth and thirst-quenching. Just remember to drink it as soon as you have made it or to refrigerate and keep for the minimum possible time.

Yield: 1 litre (1¾ pints/4 cups)

seeds of 6–8 pomegranates

caster (superfine) sugar, to taste

a few whole ice cubes, to serve

mint leaves, to decorate

Put the pomegranate seeds in a blender or food processor and whizz to a liquid. Add sugar to taste.

Serve with a few ice cubes and decorate with some mint leaves.

Tartare di merluzzo con limone confit e melograno
Cod tartare with preserved lemon and pomegranate seeds

The cod in this recipe allows me to combine some very characterful ingredients – lemon verbena, coriander seeds, pomegranate seeds and lemon confit. The result is perfect as a small starter or as a main course with attitude.

Serves 6

2 sprigs of lemon verbena, plus extra to garnish

2 sprigs of flat-leaf parsley

2 spring onions (scallions)

600g (1¼lb) skinless cod fillet

2 tsp coriander seeds

120g (scant 4oz/scant 1 cup) pomegranate seeds

3 tbsp extra virgin olive oil

salt and freshly ground black pepper

for the preserved lemons

5 or 6 unwaxed lemons

2–3 tsp coarse salt

Make the preserved lemons a month in advance. Wash and dry the lemons, then cut them in quarters lengthways, leaving them joined at the top. Sprinkle the inside of each lemon with ½ tsp coarse salt. Transfer to a large jar and put a weight on top that is heavy enough to press the lemons down so they release some of their juices. Seal the jar and store in a cool dry place for 1 month before using.

To make the cod tartare, carefully wash and dry the lemon verbena and parsley, then chop coarsely. Peel and trim the spring onions (scallions), then chop finely. Cut the cod into slices, then chop roughly. In a bowl, mix together the fish, lemon verbena and parsley, spring onions (scallions), coriander seeds and pomegranate seeds. Add the olive oil and salt and pepper to taste, then mix together well. Serve with some zest of preserved lemon and some lemon verbena.

Insalata di fagiolini verdi con aglio brasato e melograno, vinaigrette al sidro
Green bean salad with garlic, pomegranate seeds and cider

Whatever you serve this salad with, the result is always enjoyable. The braised garlic adds roundness and fragrance to the vegetables without overpowering them, and the thyme, cider and pomegranate seeds really enhance their taste. As far as I am concerned, garlic is very good for the soul.

Serves 6

2 handfuls of baby spinach leaves

600g (1¼lb) French beans

1 head of garlic

50ml (2fl oz/scant ¼ cup) extra virgin olive oil, plus extra to drizzle

sprig of thyme

50ml (2fl oz/scant ¼ cup) cider

120g (scant 4oz/scant 1 cup) pomegranate seeds

salt and freshly ground black pepper

Wash and dry the spinach well, then set aside. Wash the beans and trim the ends. Bring a pan of salted water to the boil over a high heat, add the trimmed beans, reduce the heat and cook for 10–12 minutes, until al dente. Drain, cool and set aside.

Preheat the oven to 180°C (350°F/Gas 4). Put the head of garlic in a small pan with enough cold water to cover it. Bring to the boil over a high heat, then drain. Repeat 2 more times, then drain well. Put the garlic on a piece of tinfoil, drizzle with a little olive oil and add the sprig of thyme. Enclose the garlic in the foil and cook in the preheated oven for 10 minutes. Remove from the oven, open the parcel and leave to cool.

Meanwhile, put the rest of the olive oil and the cider in a bowl with a pinch of salt and pepper and mix well.

Mix the cooked beans, spinach and pomegranate seeds in a serving dish, add the cider vinaigrette and toss well. To serve, pull 3 cloves of garlic from the cooked head and, without peeling them, cut into halves and arrange on top of the salad.

Boulette di formaggio con uvetta e melograno
Cheese bites with dried fruit and pomegranate seeds

This is a classic life-saving recipe that can be put together quickly for those moments when taste and presentation really matter. Must be tried!

Serves 6

300g (10oz/generous 1 cup) soft goat's cheese

50g (2oz/scant ⅔ cup) grated Parmesan cheese

45g (1½oz/generous ¼ cup) sultanas (golden raisins), soaked in water, then squeezed dry

100g (3½oz/generous ¾ cup cups) pomegranate seeds

salt and freshly ground black pepper

Put the goat's cheese, Parmesan cheese and sultanas (golden raisins) in a bowl and add a little salt and pepper to taste.

Cover with clingfilm (plastic wrap) and leave in the refrigerator to rest for 20 minutes. Roll small quantities of the cheese mixture between your hands to make balls, then roll the balls in the pomegranate seeds, pressing the seeds lightly into the cheese so they stick.

Refrigerate until ready to serve cold as an aperitif.

Crema di patate dolci speziata con tuile di Parmigiano al melograno
Spicy sweet potato soup with parmesan and pomegranate tuiles

The sweet potato in this recipe gives a constant note of background sweetness to the decisive taste of the tuiles, and the cumin seeds manage to tie all the different tastes together.

Serves 6

900g (1¾lb) sweet potatoes

1 onion

1 garlic clove

3 tbsp delicate extra virgin olive oil

2 tsp cumin seeds, plus extra to garnish

1.5 litres (2½ pints/6⅓ cups) vegetable stock

125g (4oz/½ cup) natural yogurt

salt and freshly ground black pepper

1 leek, green part only, thinly sliced, to garnish

for the tuiles

60g (2½oz) Parmesan cheese, thinly shaved

30g (1oz/¼ cup) pomegranate seeds

Make the tuiles. Preheat the oven to 180°C (350°F/Gas 4) and line a baking sheet with baking parchment (parchment paper). Put a tian ring on the paper and put a few Parmesan shavings and pomegranate seeds inside the ring to form a thin layer. Carefully remove the ring and repeat a further 5 times, until the Parmesan cheese and pomegranate seeds have all been used. Place the baking sheet in the preheated oven and bake for 5 minutes, until the cheese melts into pale golden tuiles. Remove from the oven and leave until completely cool.

Meanwhile, peel the sweet potatoes and cut into small cubes. Peel and finely slice the onion and garlic. Heat the olive oil in a flameproof casserole dish over a medium heat, add the onion, garlic and cumin seeds and cook for 3 minutes, until the onion has softened. Add the sweet potato cubes and cook for 5 minutes more, stirring frequently to ensure they do not stick.

Bring the vegetable stock to the boil in a pan over a medium heat, then add the boiling stock to the casserole containing the sweet potatoes. Add salt to taste. Reduce the heat and cook for 20 minutes more, until the sweet potatoes are tender. Transfer to a food processor and whizz briefly to purée. Stir in the yogurt and sprinkle with pepper. Divide between 6 hot bowls, garnish with a few thin strips of leek and some cumin seeds, then serve with the cheese and pomegranate tuiles.

What would you compare a pomegranate to? I have always

thought it resembles a coffer full of vermilion red rubies. This ancient and extraordinary fruit has always fascinated the peoples who cultivated it and it came to acquire symbolic and religious meanings in many cultures. The ancient Egyptians used to place pomegranates in tombs, in Greek mythology the seeds of the fruit caused Persephone to become the prisoner of Hades, god of the underworld, while the Koran mentions pomegranates among the fruits to be found in Paradise. The originality and allure of the pomegranate have also won it a place in our modern society. In the kitchen it is used today to accompany the most varied recipes; its sharp, sweet taste goes perfectly well with cheese, fish, sweet and sour dishes and desserts. It has, in addition, remarkable decorative qualities, given that pomegranate seeds add a bright and colourful touch to any dish. For all these reasons it is a fruit that has always fired my imagination, to the extent that I have created a whole series of dishes entirely around its seeds. The best pomegranates are the ones that are heaviest in proportion to their size, as that is a sign that they are full of juice, while the largest of all tend to have the sweetest pulp.

Tabulè con melanzane e melograno
Tabbouleh with aubergines and pomegranate seeds

Like every salad, tabbouleh can be made with a myriad of ingredients. This version is an amalgam of all my favourite things: the bitterness of the aubergines (eggplants) is tempered by the sweetness of the figs, and both go well with the freshness of the mint, the zest of the grated lemon and the tart sweetness of fresh pomegranates.

Serves 6

1 aubergine (eggplant)

2 tbsp extra virgin olive oil

1 garlic clove, unpeeled

80g (3oz/scant ½ cup) dried figs, cut into small pieces

1 tbsp finely chopped flat-leaf parsley

1 tsp finely chopped mint leaves

zest of ½ lemon, grated

300g (10oz/1½ cups) couscous

125g (4oz/1 cup) pomegranate seeds, plus extra to garnish

salt and freshly ground black pepper

Wash and dry the aubergine (eggplant, then cut into medium-sized cubes. Place on a rack, sprinkle with salt and leave for 30 minutes so the bitter juices are drawn out. Dry the aubergine (eggplant) cubes with paper towels, wiping away the juices.

Heat 1 tbsp of the olive oil in a frying pan over a medium heat, add the garlic and aubergine (eggplant) cubes and fry for 7 minutes, until they start to take on a golden colour. Reduce the heat, discard the garlic and add the dried figs. Cook for 3 minutes, then remove from the heat and add the chopped parsley and mint and the lemon zest to the pan. Add salt and pepper to taste and leave to rest.

Meanwhile, cook the couscous according to the packet instructions in double its volume of boiling salted water, until all the water has been absorbed. Stir in the remaining oil, then add the aubergines (eggplants) and figs and mix well. Stir in the pomegranate seeds. Press the mixture firmly into 6 moulds, then turn them out, top with pomegranate seeds and serve.

Pomegranates

Dolce di tagliatelle
Tagliatelle pudding

This is one of those puddings that I love to make because the recipe is so amenable. If a couple of extra almonds fall in the bowl it doesn't matter. Whatever you do to it, it will prove a great success!

Serves 6–8

50g (2oz/scant ⅓ cup) sultanas (golden raisins)

300g (10oz/2 cups) 00 flour, sifted, plus extra for dusting

50g (2oz/scant ¼ cup) unsalted butter, softened and diced, plus extra for greasing and for dotting

3 eggs

pinch of salt

150g (5oz/scant 1 cup) almonds, blanched, peeled and chopped

200g (7oz/scant 1 cup) caster (superfine) sugar

1 tbsp orange-flower water

zest of 1 unwaxed lemon, finely grated

90ml (scant 3½fl oz/ generous ⅓ cup) orange liqueur (such as Cointreau or Grand Marnier)

Preheat the oven to 180°C (350°F/Gas 4). Soak the sultanas (golden raisins) for 30 minutes in hot water, then squeeze them dry. Meanwhile, heap the flour on a work surface, make a well in the centre and add the butter, eggs and salt. Mix the ingredients to form a smooth dough.

Roll out the pasta on a floured surface to make a thin sheet. Leave to rest for 10–15 minutes.

Put the chopped almonds in a mixing bowl with the sugar, the softened sultanas (golden raisins), the orange-flower water and the grated lemon zest. Combine thoroughly.

Cut the sheet of pasta into tagliatelle.

Grease a 25cm (10in) diameter cake tin (pan) and dust with flour. Place a layer of tagliatelle on the bottom of the tin (pan) and scatter some of the almond mixture over the top. Add a few drops of the orange liqueur followed by a few dots of butter. Repeat the layers of tagliatelle and almond mixture until all the almond mixture is used up, finishing with a layer of tagliatelle.

Cover with tinfoil, place in the preheated oven and cook for 1 hour, until golden and crispy.

Serve warm.

Risotto alla Parmigiana con tartufo
Risotto parmigiana with truffle

Whichever truffle you use, it must be fresh, and don't use truffle oils or cheeses because they are full of chemicals. This famous *risotto alla Parmigiana* is so good that it is delicious even if you do not add any truffle!

Serves 6

80g (3oz/scant ⅓ cup) unsalted butter

1 onion, peeled and finely chopped

1.5 litres (2½ pints/6⅓ cups) lightly salted chicken stock

550g (1lb 2oz/2¾ cups) Carnaroli or Vialone risotto rice

100ml (3½fl oz/scant ½ cup) dry white wine

70g (scant 3oz/generous ¾ cup) grated Parmesan cheese

50g (2oz) fragrant, ripe white truffle

Melt half the butter in a large pan over a gentle heat, add the onion and cook for 3 minutes, stirring occasionally and taking care not to brown it.

Meanwhile, bring the stock to the boil in another pan over a medium heat.

Increase the heat a little under the softened onion, add the rice and cook for 2 minutes, stirring continuously. Add the wine and continue to cook until the wine evaporates, then start adding the boiling stock, a little at a time. Stir after each addition and continue stirring.

When all the stock has been added and a few minutes before the rice is cooked, add the grated Parmesan cheese. Continue to stir.

Cut the truffle into fine shavings.

When the rice is cooked but still al dente, take the pan off the heat. Add the remaining butter and stir well.

Serve very hot with plenty of truffle shavings.

Gran bollito misto con mostarda piccante di frutta
Boiled meat platter with spicy fruit mustard

This is my version of a traditional Italian regional dish; your version may be different, depending on the meats you like and what your butcher has available. The most important rule to follow is to stick to the different cooking times for the meats. PICTURED OVERLEAF

Serves 6–8

6 celery sticks

6 carrots

6 white onions, peeled and stuck with a few cloves

3 small bunches of flat-leaf parsley

500g (1lb) rump (top round) steak

500g (1lb) brisket of veal

½ tongue

500g (1lb) calf's head

a few pieces of oxtail

1 ox cheek

1 knuckle of veal

½ boiling fowl or chicken

coarse salt

mixed spicy fruit mustard, to serve (see p.158)

Fill 3 large pans with water and add salt to each.

Wash the celery and peel the carrots.

Put 2 celery sticks, 2 carrots, 2 onions stuck with cloves and a small bunch of parsley in each pan. Put 1 pan over a high heat and bring to the boil. When the water is boiling, reduce the heat to a simmer and add the rump steak.

After 1 hour, add the brisket of veal and bring the other 2 pans to the boil.

When these come to the boil, reduce the heat to a simmer and add the tongue and calf's head to one pan, and the oxtail, ox cheek and knuckle of veal to the other pan.

After another hour, add the boiling fowl or chicken to the pan containing the steak and the brisket of veal.

Continue to simmer all 3 pans for 1½ hours more.

Test for doneness with a carving fork: the fork should sink easily into the meat. Keep testing for doneness as cooking times vary so much.

As soon as the meats are ready, remove them from the pan with a slotted spoon.

Slice them and arrange on large, heated serving dishes. Sprinkle with coarse salt and ladle plenty of the cooking liquor over the top. Serve immediately with the spicy fruit mustard.

Linguine con ragout di pistacchi e scampi
Linguine with pistachio purée and scampi

This is one of those recipes where the quality of the fresh ingredients can really make a difference. There is no doubt that the scampi must be really fresh, but you should also take care to buy the very best pistachio nuts.

Serves 6

24 raw scampi, in the shell

1 tbsp sultanas (golden raisins) soaked for 15 minutes in cold water then patted dry

1 tbsp salted capers, rinsed and soaked for 5 minutes in cold water then patted dry

150g (5oz/1 cup) pistachio nuts, shelled

50ml (2fl oz/scant ¼ cup) extra virgin olive oil

500g (1lb) linguine pasta

salt

Wash and peel the scampi and remove the heads, carefully removing the black filaments. Refrigerate until required.

Bring a large pan of salted water to the boil over a high heat.

Meanwhile, put the sultanas (golden raisins) and capers in a blender with the pistachio nuts and olive oil and whizz together to form a purée. Transfer the pistachio nut purée to a deep non-stick frying pan.

Add the pasta to the boiling salted water in the large pan, having first taken a ladleful of the water to add to the pistachio nut purée. Reduce the heat under the pasta pan and cook for 10–13 minutes, until the pasta is al dente.

Two minutes before the pasta is ready, put the pan containing the pistachio nut purée over a medium heat. Add the scampi and salt to taste. Stir occasionally to warm through.

When the pasta is ready, strain and add to the pistachio and scampi mixture. Toss well for 1 minute, then serve immediately.

Spaghetti con olio, aglio, acciughe fresche e noci
Spaghetti with oil, garlic, anchovies and walnuts

I wanted this recipe to capture all the characteristics and flavour of the anchovy. I hope you agree that the contrast with the slightly bitter taste of the walnuts works really well. PICTURED ON PAGE 127

Serves 6

18 fresh anchovies

4 salted anchovies

2 garlic cloves

50ml (2fl oz/scant ¼ cup) extra virgin olive oil

90g (3½oz/scant 1 cup) shelled walnuts

500g (1lb) spaghetti

salt

chilli powder, to serve (optional)

for the garnish

6 fresh anchovies

1 tbsp extra virgin olive oil

wild fennel fronds

Clean the fresh anchovies, removing the heads and the innards. Split them open and remove the spines. Leave 6 anchovies whole and cut the others into small pieces. Rinse the salted anchovies.

Peel the garlic, cut it in half and put it in a frying pan over a medium heat with the olive oil. Once the garlic has turned golden, discard it and add the salted anchovies to the pan. Reduce the heat and stir continuously until the anchovies have broken up and are reduced to a paste.

Bring a large pan of salted water to the boil over a high heat. Meanwhile, add the chopped fresh anchovies to the salted anchovy paste and cook for 2 minutes, then add the whole anchovies, taking care not to break them. Finally add the walnuts. Cook for 1 minute, then remove from the heat and set aside.

When the salted water has come to the boil, add the spaghetti, reduce the heat and cook for 9–11 minutes, until al dente.

Meanwhile, prepare the garnish. Clean the anchovies, remove their heads and innards, then split them in half lengthways. Heat the olive oil in a small frying pan over a medium heat, add the anchovies and fry for a maximum of 1 minute on each side.

Drain the spaghetti thoroughly, add to the anchovy mixture and combine thoroughly. Divide between 6 serving bowls, garnish with the whole anchovy and the fennel fronds, then sprinkle with a little chilli powder, if liked.

Moleche fritte
Deep-fried soft-shell crabs

'*Moleche*' is Venetian dialect for the male of the common crab when, in spring and again in autumn, it is changing its shell and is soft enough to be eaten whole. They are a seasonal speciality in New York.

Serves 6

30 live soft-shell crabs

200g (7oz/1⅓ cups) 00 flour

peanut or rapeseed oil, for deep-frying

salt

Carefully wash, then dry the soft-shell crabs, taking care to cut off the ends of the claws. Place the flour on a plate and dip the crabs in the flour.

Put the peanut or rapeseed oil in a deep pan over a medium heat and heat to no more than 170°C (340°F). Deep-fry the crabs in the hot oil until they are cooked through and golden brown. Remove with a slotted spoon and drain on paper towels. Add salt to taste and serve immediately.

Crema fredda di fagioli borlotti e basilico
Chilled cream of borlotti bean and basil soup

This is my version of the classic *zuppa di fagioli*; I often serve it for Sunday lunch in early autumn when we can still eat outside around the big table under the old sycamore tree. The fresh-tasting basil and the fragrance of the extra virgin olive oil make a really pleasing creamed soup, and this cold version is delicious.
PICTURED ON PAGE 121

Serves 6

1kg (2lb) borlotti beans, shelled, or 500g (1lb/2½ cups) dried borlotti beans, soaked overnight in cold water and rinsed

2 celery sticks, diced

2 carrots, diced

1 garlic clove, peeled and finely sliced

1 onion, finely sliced

5 black peppercorns

1 ham bone

a few sprigs of basil, finely chopped, plus extra to garnish

4 tbsp extra virgin olive oil, plus extra to drizzle

salt and freshly ground black pepper

Put the beans in a large saucepan with the diced celery and carrot and the sliced garlic and onion.

Add the peppercorns, ham bone, basil and the olive oil.

Cover with cold water, bring to the boil over a high heat, reduce the heat, then simmer for 1½–2 hours, adding extra water if necessary. Add salt to taste (taking into account the saltiness of the ham bone).

When the beans are soft, remove the ham bone and whizz to a creamy consistency in a blender, reserving a few to garnish.

Return the puréed beans to the pan and cook for 1 hour more, adding more water as necessary. Remove from the heat, leave to cool, then refrigerate until cold.

Serve with a drizzle of oil and garnish with a few basil leaves, the reserved cooked beans and a sprinkle of black pepper.

Focaccia all'olio d'oliva e rosmarino
Focaccia with olive oil and rosemary

This is the traditional recipe for the *a fügassa*, the well-known Genoese focaccia. I have added rosemary, which I really love; I hope the Genoese people don't object to it. This focaccia is so deeply rooted in their food culture that it is now a Slow Food Presidium. PICTURED ON PAGE 120

Makes 1 x 500g (1lb) loaf

30g (1oz) fresh brewer's yeast

300ml (½ pint/scant 1¼ cup) warm water

1 tsp caster (superfine) sugar

500g (1lb/3⅓ cups) 00 flour

½ tsp salt

300ml (½ pint/scant 1¼ cup) extra virgin olive oil, plus extra for greasing

100ml (3½fl oz/scant ½ cup) water

a few sprigs of rosemary

coarse salt, for sprinkling

Dissolve the yeast in the warm water with the sugar. Sift the flour into a bowl with the salt, make a well in the centre and add 100ml (3½fl oz/scant ½ cup) of the olive oil and the yeast mixture. Knead thoroughly until the dough is soft and stretchy.

Wrap in a clean cloth and leave to prove in a warm, draught-free place for 2 hours, until the dough has doubled in size.

Oil a rectangular baking sheet, then stretch the dough out evenly to cover the base.

Whisk together the remaining olive oil and the water and use to paint the surface of the dough. Leave to prove again for 1 hour.

Meanwhile, preheat the oven to 200°C (400°F/Gas 6). Sprinkle the dough with rosemary leaves and a little coarse salt, place in the preheated oven and bake for 15–20 minutes, until the surface is golden. Remove from the baking sheet and leave to cool. Serve warm, cut into pieces.

These are recipes which I find appropriate for the mild beginning of the autumn, when we are not yet inclined to give thought to the rigours of winter ahead. For the time being we can still enjoy the weather: it is clement enough for us to continue to lay the Sunday lunch table under the big sycamore. It is true that we have to be prepared to suffer the odd shiver, but the pleasurable experience far outweighs that slight discomfort. In our region, early autumn is normally temperate and pleasant, and there are many days when the tail of summer still threads its way through the new season. The weather is therefore perfect for us and a group of friends to continue to enjoy a meal *al fresco*. At this time of year I love to prepare dishes with a dual spirit, such as a cream of bean soup served cold and scented with basil, beef served raw in the form of a carpaccio, or the seasonal, deep-fried, soft-shell crabs which we eat instead of a classic fish dish, simplifying it and making it closer to something akin to fish fingers (sticks). These are dishes which do not desire to conform fully to the typically autumnal table but are happy to remain on the threshold of the season, just as we are.

Carpaccio di cervo con salsa ai ribes rossi
Venison carpaccio with redcurrant sauce

If you have a good butcher, ask him to slice the fillet of venison really thinly for you. The secret of this recipe, over and above the fact that the meat should be well hung and of good quality, is the paper-thin cut, which allows you to enjoy the full flavour and tenderness of the venison.

Serves 6

540g (1lb 2oz) venison fillet

for the redcurrant sauce
500g (1lb) redcurrants
100ml (3½fl oz/scant ½ cup) white wine vinegar
½ tsp ground cinnamon
1 clove
150g (5oz/scant ¾ cup) caster (superfine) sugar

to serve
salt
extra virgin olive oil

To make the redcurrant sauce, wash and pat dry the redcurrants with paper towels.

Make a marinade with the vinegar, cinnamon and clove. Put the redcurrants in a bowl and pour the marinade over. Marinate for 3 hours.

Prepare the venison by wrapping it in clingfilm (plastic wrap) and putting it in the freezer for 2–3 hours. This will make it easier to slice. Meanwhile, transfer the redcurrants and the marinade to a saucepan and bring to the boil over a medium heat. Reduce the heat and cook for 15 minutes. Skim off any froth, then add the sugar and cook for 15 minutes more. Remove from the heat and leave to cool.

When you are ready to serve the dish, remove the venison from the freezer, remove the clingfilm (plastic wrap) and slice as thinly as you can.

Serve the carpaccio very cold with a pinch of salt, a drizzle of oil and the redcurrant sauce.

Autumn comfort

Tatin aux poires Pear tart tatin

This sounds a bit like its famous French cousin, tarte Tatin, and in fact the method is very similar. Its simplicity enhances the taste of good-quality fruit and it is, of all the tarts I make, my favourite. I think the pears framed by the pastry look really beautiful. You could try adding some soaked and dried sultanas, and perhaps a dusting of cinnamon to finish.

Serves 6–8

6 Williams pears or similar

100g (3½oz/scant ½ cup) unsalted butter, softened

80g (3oz/generous ⅓ cup) caster (superfine) sugar

for the pastry (pie dough)

250g (8oz/1⅔ cups) 00 flour, plus extra for dusting

150g (5oz/scant ⅔ cup) unsalted butter, softened and diced

pinch of salt

2–3 tbsp iced water

Make the pastry (pie dough). Sift the flour into a bowl and make a well in the centre. Add the softened butter and salt. Rub the butter into the flour using your fingertips until it resembles coarse breadcrumbs. Add 1 tbsp iced water at a time and blend it in to make a smooth, soft dough. Wrap in clingfilm (plastic wrap) and refrigerate for at least 1 hour.

Preheat the oven to 200°C (400°F/Gas 6). Peel the pears, cut in half and remove the cores. Spread the butter over the base of a 24cm (9½in) diameter cake tin (pan), then sprinkle over the sugar. Arrange the pears on top, cut side down, then put the tin (pan) over a low heat for 8–10 minutes, until the sugar has melted and caramelized. Remove from the heat and transfer to the preheated oven. Cook for 15 minutes.

Meanwhile, roll out the pastry (pie dough) on a lightly floured surface to make a circle that is slightly larger than the diameter of the tin (pan). Remove the tin (pan) from the oven and lay the pastry (pie dough) on top of the pears. Use a fork to gently press any excess pastry (pie dough) down into the tin (pan). Prick the surface of the pastry (pie dough), return the tin (pan) to the oven and cook for 15 minutes more, until the pastry (pie dough) is cooked and has become light gold in colour. Remove the tart from the oven and leave for no more than 3 minutes before turning it out, pastry (pie dough) face down, onto a plate. Serve hot.

Schiaccia all'uva
Grape 'schiaccia'

This classic autumn recipe comes from Tuscany. It is made at harvest time when the grapes destined for wine-making are good, firm, sweet and in plentiful supply. The secret is to use wine-making grapes, which are quite different from dessert grapes.

Makes 1 x 500g (1lb) loaf

25g (1oz) fresh brewer's yeast

250ml (8fl oz/1 cup) warm water

500g (1lb/3⅓ cups) 00 flour, plus extra for dusting

5 tbsp caster (superfine) sugar

1 tbsp extra virgin olive oil, plus extra for brushing

1kg (2lb) black grapes

unsalted butter, for greasing

Dissolve the yeast in the water. Sift the flour into a bowl, make a well in the centre and add the yeast, 2 tbsp of the sugar and the olive oil. Bring the ingredients together and knead to make a soft, smooth dough. Transfer to a clean bowl, cover with a clean cloth and leave to prove in a warm place for 1 hour.

Wash the grapes, remove from the stem and dry with paper towels. Grease a baking sheet. Roll out just over half the dough on a floured surface to a thickness of 2cm (¾in, then transfer to the prepared baking sheet. Cover the dough with grapes, reserving a handful for later use. Sprinkle with 2 tbsp of the sugar.

Roll out the remaining dough to a thickness of 1cm (½in) and lay it on top of the grapes. Pinch the edges of the dough together to seal, then leave to prove for 1 hour more.

Preheat the oven to 200°C (400°F/Gas 6). Prick the surface of the bread with a fork and top with the remaining grapes. Brush lightly with the rest of the olive oil, sprinkle with 1 tbsp of the sugar, then place in the preheated oven and bake for 45 minutes, until brown and crusty. Serve warm or cold.

Salsa al vino per formaggi stagionati
Wine relish to accompany mature cheese

This sauce is synonymous with good food and getting together around the table with friends. The tradition of serving it with cheese comes from Northern Italy. The sauce envelops a sliver of cheese in a thousand flavours. Enjoy it as you drink a glass of good red wine, watch the sun set and wallow in everyone's company.

Yield: 250ml (8fl oz/1 cup)

500ml (17fl oz/2 cups) red wine

120g (scant 4oz/generous ½ cup) caster (superfine) sugar

2 pieces of orange zest

4 star anise

1 cinnamon stick

3 cloves

pinch of salt

½ tsp cornflour (cornstarch) dissolved in 1 tbsp water

Put the wine, sugar, orange zest, spices and salt in a saucepan over a medium heat and bring to the boil. Reduce the heat to low and simmer for 15 minutes. Remove from the heat and add the cornflour (cornstarch) mixture.

Stir well and leave to cool and thicken. Serve with mature (sharp) cheeses.

Compote di petto d'oca con arancia candita al cavolo confit
Goose breast with candied orange and red cabbage

Goose breast looks and tastes lovely when served like this. It is great for anyone who enjoys a morsel of something good rather than a whole plateful. I serve it warm as an outdoor snack and for Sunday brunch.

Yield: 500ml (17fl oz/2cups)

2 knobs of unsalted butter

1 goose breast, skin on

1 small red cabbage

1 tbsp clear honey

3 tbsp caster (superfine) sugar

1 tbsp water

zest of ½ orange, cut into strips

2 tbsp red wine vinegar

salt and freshly ground black pepper

Melt 1 knob of the butter in a saucepan over a low heat, add the goose breast and cook for 12–14 minutes, stirring occasionally, until the meat is golden and crispy on the outside but still rare inside. Remove from the heat, add salt and pepper and leave to cool.

Trim off the outer leaves and the tough stalk of the cabbage, then slice very thinly. Melt the second knob of butter in a saucepan over a low heat, add the prepared cabbage and cook for 1–2 minutes. Add the honey, salt and pepper and cook for 30 minutes more, until the cabbage is soft.

Meanwhile, dissolve the sugar in a small pan with the water over a low heat. When the sugar has dissolved, increase the heat, bring to the boil and add the orange zest. Cook for 5 minutes more, then remove the zest using a spoon and transfer to a sheet of baking parchment (parchment paper). Leave to cool.

Remove the cabbage from the pan and deglaze the pan with the wine vinegar.

Cut the cooked goose breast into slices. Put a layer of cabbage in the bottom of a 500ml (17fl oz/2 cups) jar, add few slices of goose breast and some candied orange zest. Repeat until all the ingredients have been used up. Cover with the pan juices. Serve warm.

This chapter is dedicated to my husband who, year on year, produces wines which are, in his words, better and better, if not to say extraordinary. His enthusiasm warrants as much praise as his commitment but I will stop here so as to spare you the long list of compliments that I will have to offer him at the next tasting. Every year I find myself unwillingly drawn into the 'vineyard lotto' – a tediously extensive series of forecasts aimed at determining the best dates for the grape harvest. I shall not go into the question of whether, in past years, the fault with the wine lay in the forecast or with whoever made it, nor am I interested in discussing the quality of the 'nectar'. Instead, my true interest lies in the annual organization of the grape-picking team. This is a disorganized cluster of unskilled labourers who wander around the vineyard apparently with no clear purpose. I recruit only our closest and most trusted friends to the team because the real goal of the venture is to enjoy together the great, almost ritual, tea that I prepare afterwards to raise their spirits after all their efforts. Normally, someone else comes along on the following day to do the real job of harvesting.

Tartellette all'uva bianca, porri, formaggio fresco di capra
Grape, leek and goat's cheese tartlets

These little tarts are the 'polite' version of the well-known *torta salata*. Personally I prefer to make these little ones; they look pretty and make a great alternative to something sweet as a snack.

Serves 6

for the pastry (pie dough)
500g (1lb/3⅓ cups) 00 flour, plus extra for dusting
300g (10oz/scant 1¼ cups) unsalted butter, softened and diced, plus extra for greasing
pinch of salt
2–3 tbsp iced water

for the filling
2 leeks
1 tbsp extra virgin olive oil
2 eggs
300ml (½ pint/scant 1¼ cups) single (light) cream
100g (3½oz/generous ⅓ cup) soft goat's cheese
50g (2oz/scant ⅔ cup) grated Parmesan cheese
9 green grapes, halved
salt, to taste

Make the pastry (pie dough). Sift the flour into a bowl and make a well in the centre. Add the softened butter and salt. Rub the butter into the flour using your fingertips until it resembles breadcrumbs. Add 1 tbsp iced water at a time and blend it in to make a smooth soft dough. Refrigerate for at least 1 hour.

Meanwhile, make the filling. Clean the leeks, removing any tough outer layers and any tough green parts, then slice the tender white parts thinly. Heat the olive oil in a frying pan over a medium heat, add the sliced leek and cook for 5–6 minutes, until soft, stirring frequently to ensure it does not burn. Remove from the heat, salt lightly and leave to cool.

Put the eggs in a bowl with the cream and mix together gently using a fork. Add the goat's cheese and Parmesan and stir well until smooth. Stir in the cooled leeks.

Preheat the oven to 200°C (400°F/Gas 6) and grease 6 tartlet tins (pans). Roll out the pastry (pie dough) on a floured surface and cut 6 rounds to fit the tins (pans). Line the tins (pans) with the pastry (pie dough), fill with dried beans, then place in the preheated oven and cook for 5 minutes, until the pastry (pie dough) starts to firm up, but does not colour.

Remove the pastry (pie dough) cases from the oven, discard the beans and fill the cases with the leek and cheese mixture. Decorate each with 3 grape halves and return to the oven for 20 minutes, until set. Serve with Grape Jelly (see p.83)

Vineyard picnic

Pere al vino
Pears in wine

Certain recipes and tastes become indelibly associated with a time of year. Here in Asolo, when we smell the heady scent of mulled wine as we walk along our arcaded pavements, it is a clear signal that we are in for our first misty autumn mornings. For me this recipe evokes those memories.

Serves 6

6 small firm-fleshed pears (such as Williams)

500ml (17fl oz/2 cups) full-bodied red wine

100g (3½oz/½ cup) sugar

2 cloves

½ cinnamon stick

2 star anise

Peel the pears and put in a flameproof casserole dish with the wine, sugar, cloves, cinnamon stick and star anise. Cover and bring the wine to the boil over a high heat. Reduce the heat to the minimum and cook for 30 minutes, or until the pears are cooked through but still firm. When the pears are ready, remove from the casserole dish, increase the heat and cook to reduce the wine until it is thick and syrupy.

Serve the pears warm with the warm wine sauce. If preferred, you can serve the pears cold, reheating the sauce gently before serving.

Torta al caramello con salsa ai frutti rossi
Toffee torta with berry sauce

This is actually a traditional Portuguese recipe but the original can be a bit on the dry side. That is why I decided to serve it with a really liquid red berry sauce. I think the slightly tart, refined taste of the berries is perfect with the flavour of the caramel.

Serves 6

200g (7oz/generous ¾ cup) unsalted butter, softened, plus extra for greasing

250g (8oz/1⅔ cups) 00 flour, sifted, plus extra for dusting

125ml (4fl oz/½ cup) milk

125ml (4fl oz/½ cup) single (light) cream

200g (7oz/scant 1 cup) caster (superfine) sugar

3 eggs

½ tsp vanilla extract

1 tsp baking powder

for the berry sauce

500g (1lb/3⅓ cups) mixed berries (raspberries and blueberries)

30g (1oz/generous ⅛ cup) caster (superfine) sugar

Preheat the oven to 180°C (350°F/Gas 4). Grease and flour a 25cm (10in) diameter cake tin (pan). Mix the milk and cream together.

Put the sugar in a saucepan over a low heat and cook for 10–15 minutes, stirring frequently until the sugar is a golden caramel colour. Add the milk and cream and mix well, taking care as the caramel may splash. Remove from the heat and leave to cool.

When the mixture is cool, add the butter and stir well. Add the eggs, one at a time, then the vanilla. Continue stirring until the mixture begins to thicken, then add the sifted flour and baking powder. Continue stirring until the mixture is thick and creamy.

Pour into the prepared cake tin (pan) and cook in the preheated oven for 35–40 minutes. The cake should be golden brown outside and moist inside. Remove from the oven and leave to cool.

Meanwhile, make the sauce. Wash and dry the fruit. Reserve a handful of fruit and put the rest in a pan with the sugar over a low heat. Cook gently until the sugar dissolves and the fruit starts to break up. Leave to cool, then add the reserved fruit and mix together. Serve the torta with the sauce.

Gelatina di cachi con caramello, cioccolato salato e chantilly
Persimmon jelly with caramel, salted chocolate and chantilly cream

This recipe offers a merry-go-round of flavours and textures – the persimmon jelly (jello), the bitter, slightly salty chocolate, the crunchiness of the caramel and the final leap into the ethereal Chantilly cream.

Serves 6

for the persimmon jelly (jello)
1.5kg (3lb) ripe persimmons
500ml (17fl oz/2 cups) water
50ml (2fl oz/scant ¼ cup) white rum
500g (1lb/generous 2¼cups) caster (superfine) sugar
25g (1oz) leaf gelatine

for the salted chocolate
150g (5oz) 75% plain chocolate
a few Maldon salt flakes

for the caramel
150g (5oz/scant ¾ cup) caster (superfine) sugar
a few drops of lemon juice

for the Chantilly cream
500ml (17fl oz/2 cups) double (heavy) cream
100g (3½oz/½ cup) caster (superfine) sugar

Wash the persimmons, scoop out the flesh and put it through a food mill, fine sieve or potato ricer.

Put the water, rum and sugar in a saucepan over a high heat, stir and bring to the boil. Reduce the heat, add the persimmon flesh and cook for 15 minutes more. Meanwhile, soak the gelatine in cold water for 10 minutes.

Leave the persimmon mixture to cool, then add the soaked and squeezed-out gelatine. Stir until the gelatine has completely dissolved, then pour into 6 small serving glasses and refrigerate.

To make the salted chocolate discs, cut the chocolate into small pieces, place in a bain-marie over a medium heat and stir from time to time until the chocolate has melted to a smooth, runny consistency.

Divide the melted chocolate between 6 silicone, round-bottomed mini jelly moulds (jello molds) or pudding basins, adding a little at a time. The chocolate should cover the base of the mould with a thin layer. Leave to harden slightly, then sprinkle with a few salt flakes. Leave to set completely.

Meanwhile, make the caramel. Heat the sugar in a pan over a high heat with a few drops of lemon juice. When the sugar starts to caramelize, reduce the heat until it turns a golden caramel colour. Repeat the method as for the chocolate discs, pouring the sugar into another 6 moulds to make a layer of caramel on the bottom of each. Leave to harden.

When the jellies (jellos) have set and you are almost ready to serve the dish, make the Chantilly cream. Put the cream in a bowl with the sugar and beat well to form soft peaks. Spoon into a serving dish. To serve, carefully take the chocolate and caramel discs out of their moulds. Put 1 caramel disc on each jelly followed by 1 chocolate disc. Serve accompanied by the Chantilly cream.

Castagne caramellate
Caramelized chestnuts

We use *marrone* chestnuts to make this kind of recipe in Italy; they are sweeter and have more flavour than the run-of-the-mill kind. What is more, they are much easier to peel than other varieties.

Serves 6–8

1kg (2lb) large chestnuts
1 vanilla pod (bean), split lengthways
1 bay leaf
50g (2oz/scant ¼ cup) unsalted butter
150g (5oz/scant ¾ cup) caster (superfine) sugar
150ml (¼ pint/scant ⅔ cup) dark rum

Put the chestnuts, vanilla pod (bean) and bay leaf in a pan with enough cold water to cover. Bring to the boil over a medium heat, then reduce the heat and cook for 5–8 minutes, until the chestnuts are cooked inside.

Remove from the heat and leave for 2–3 minutes to allow the flavours to infuse. Drain the chestnuts and leave to cool, then peel.

Melt the butter and sugar together in a large clean pan over a low heat, stirring continuously. When the butter and sugar have completely dissolved and the mixture is smooth, add the chestnuts. Continue to cook for 3–4 minutes, shaking the pan firmly from time to time, until the sauce has reduced. Add the rum, increase the heat and cook for 2 minutes, shaking the pan continuously until the sauce has caramelized. Serve warm.

Insalata di patate chips e cipolla fritta
Potato chip and deep-fried onion ring salad

Everyone has three potatoes and two onions in the house, don't they? And if they are really lucky, a handful of salad leaves may be lurking in the vegetable drawer. With this recipe you won't die from hunger ever again.

Serves 6

300g (10oz) baby salad leaves (salad greens)

3 potatoes, unpeeled

2 red onions

4½ tbsp extra virgin olive oil

peanut or rapeseed oil, for deep-frying

1½ tbsp red wine vinegar

sprig of oregano

salt and freshly ground black pepper

Carefully wash and dry the salad leaves (salad greens).

Wash and dry the potatoes, then use a mandolin slicer to slice them thinly. Put them in a bowl, cover with cold water and leave for 30 minutes.

Meanwhile, peel and trim the red onions and slice thinly into rings using a mandolin slicer.

Remove the potato slices from the water, drain and dry well with paper towels or a clean cloth.

Heat 1 tbsp of the olive oil in a non-stick frying pan over a medium heat and fry the potato slices, a few at a time, until crisp and golden brown on both sides. Remove with a slotted spoon and drain on paper towels. Add salt to taste.

Heat the peanut or rapeseed oil in a deep pan over a medium heat and heat to no more than 170°C (340°F). Deep-fry the onion rings in batches until golden and crisp. Remove with a slotted spoon and drain on paper towels. Add salt to taste.

To make the dressing, mix the remaining olive oil with the vinegar, a pinch of salt and the oregano leaves. Pour over the baby salad leaves (salad greens) and toss well.

To serve, add the potato chips, the fried onion rings and black pepper to taste.

Quaglie arrosto con fichi neri
Roast quail with black figs

Quail is a good place to start when choosing a meat-based main course for this time of the year. This version with black figs is delicious and very easy to make: the quail meat goes perfectly with the flavour of the figs.

Serves 6

6 ripe black figs

50g (2oz/scant ¼ cup) unsalted butter, plus 2 tbsp, softened

3 tsp 'bitter' honey, such as arbutus or chestnut honey

6 quails

6 thin slices of hard back fat or paper-thin slices of pancetta

6 juniper berries, crushed

3 garlic cloves, unpeeled

75ml (3fl oz/scant ⅓ cup) cognac

salt and freshly ground black pepper

Preheat the oven to 200°C (400°F/Gas 6). Carefully wash and dry the figs. Thoroughly mix the 2 tbsp butter with the honey in a small dish.

Make an incision in the top of the figs. Using your fingers, make the openings a little larger and fill each with 1 tsp of the butter and honey mixture.

Season the inside of the quails with salt and pepper and tie the legs together with kitchen string. Cover each quail breast with a slice of back fat or pancetta, inserting a crushed juniper berry underneath.

Melt the remaining butter in a large frying pan over a medium heat, add the unpeeled garlic and the quails and brown all over for 10 minutes. You may have to do this in batches. Discard the back fat and the juniper berries, season with salt and pepper and transfer the quails to a roasting dish.

Add the cognac to the frying pan, increase the heat and deglaze the pan, scraping up any cooking residue from the bottom. Pour these pan juices over the quails. Add the prepared figs, then place the roasting dish in the preheated oven and cook for 15 minutes, until the quails are cooked through.

Serve piping hot with the roasted figs.

Zuppa di orzo con funghi, alloro e pancetta croccante
Barley soup with mushrooms, bay leaves and bacon

The season for hot, restorative soups is back. This one makes the perfect one-dish meal. My only advice is to make the stock yourself; it won't take long. You can make it in batches and freeze it, so you have a store set by.

Serves 6

600g (1¼lb) small firm porcini mushrooms

3 tbsp extra virgin olive oil

1 onion, peeled and finely chopped

2 garlic cloves, 1 peeled and finely chopped and 1 unpeeled and crushed

2 bay leaves

1.5 litres (2½ pints/6⅓ cups) beef or mixed meat stock

375g (12oz/scant 2 cups) pearl barley

6 slices of rolled pancetta

salt and freshly ground black pepper

Clean the mushrooms, trimming the base of the stems and scraping off any soil with a small sharp knife. Try not to use water but, if absolutely necessary, clean carefully using a soft brush. Roughly chop the mushroom stalks and finely slice the caps.

Heat 2 tbsp of the olive oil in a large saucepan over a medium heat, add the chopped onion and chopped garlic and cook gently for 2–3 minutes, until golden. Add the chopped mushroom stalks and the bay leaves and cook for 2–3 minutes, stirring continuously.

Meanwhile, bring the stock to the boil in a clean saucepan over a medium heat.

Add the pearl barley to the pan with the mushroom stalks and stir well, then add the boiling stock and cook for 50 minutes, until the pearl barley is al dente.

Meanwhile, put the remaining olive oil in a non-stick frying pan over a medium heat. Add the crushed garlic clove, fry until golden, then remove from the pan and discard. Add the finely sliced mushroom caps to the pan and fry for 1–2 minutes, until golden. Remove the cooked mushroom caps with a slotted spoon to a plate and set aside.

Heat another frying pan, add the pancetta and cook until golden brown and crispy. Set aside.

When the pearl barley is ready, add the reserved mushroom caps, stir well and cook for 5 minutes more. Add salt and pepper to taste. Serve hot, topping each serving with a slice of crispy pancetta.

Insalata di funghi porcini crudi, prezzemolo e Parmigiano
Mushroom salad with parmesan

Nothing is more rewarding than the intense woodland aroma of porcini and their challenging meaty flesh. Enjoying their heady smell, hanging in the air, is one of the real pleasures of the season.

Serves 6

4 tbsp extra virgin olive oil

1 garlic clove, peeled and halved

420g (14oz) small porcini mushrooms

3 tsp lemon juice, strained

salt and freshly ground black pepper

to serve

sprigs of flat-leaf parsley

Parmesan cheese shavings

A few hours in advance, put the olive oil in a jug with the garlic.

Clean the mushrooms, trimming the base of the stems and scraping off any soil with a small sharp knife or using a soft brush. Avoid washing.

Slice the mushrooms thinly lengthways and put in a salad bowl. Add a little salt and the lemon juice and mix well.

Remove the garlic from the oil and add the resulting aromatic oil to the salad bowl. Sprinkle with pepper and leave for a minute or two.

Finely chop the parsley. Serve the mushroom salad topped with a dusting of chopped parsley and a few Parmesan shavings.

The carousel of the seasons starts to slow down, little by little. The bright, vivacious colours begin to fade, while the sun follows a new path, drawing longer and softer shadows. There is a growing desire for a certain seclusion. A new season is coming in and will swiftly impose its own pace. It is time to reorganize, to adapt to the new rhythm and, therefore, to bring warmer and softer flavours to the table. The colours of the new season are magnificent, as is the produce of the soil. In the harmonious woodlands, fragrant mushrooms are waiting to be gathered, pumpkins grow in abundance, pomegranates fill the trees and the sweetest chestnuts emerge. My garden, that magical creature, works overtime and sets us tight schedules for the picking of apples, pears, pomegranates, quinces, grapes, medlars, squashes and pumpkins. I am not sure how I manage to survive, but the experience has at least taught me to navigate my way through jams, tarts, preserves and chutneys with a certain ease, although this may be attributable more to honest enthusiasm than to a true sense of organization.

Gnocchi di zucca con funghi e salsiccia
Pumpkin gnocchi with mushrooms and sausage

Gnocchi can be truly refined. Every region of Italy has its traditional recipe but potato gnocchi from the Veneto region to Piedmont are perhaps the most famous. I am a big fan of gnocchi made with pumpkin. They are ideally suited to this autumnal sauce made with fresh sausage meat and wonderful-tasting mushrooms.

Serves 6

1.5kg (3lb) pumpkin, unpeeled, cut into wedges, deseeded and ragged bits inside discarded

1 egg

350g (12oz/2⅓cups) 00 flour, sifted, plus extra for dusting

150g (5oz) Italian sausage

200g (7oz) small firm porcini mushrooms

2 tbsp extra virgin olive oil

1 garlic clove, unpeeled and crushed

sprig of thyme

salt and freshly ground black pepper

Preheat the oven to 180°C (350°F/Gas 4). Put the pumpkin wedges in a roasting tin (pan) in the preheated oven and cook for 1 hour, until tender. Leave to cool, then peel, discard the skin and put the flesh through the fine disc of a food mill into a bowl. Add the egg, sifted flour and a pinch of salt. Mix to form a dough.

Knead the dough on a floured surface until it is smooth and firm. Take one-third of the mixture and roll it into a 'snake' 1cm (½in) in diameter. Cut into 2cm (¾in) lengths, then toss on the floured surface. Set aside in a cool place until required.

Skin the sausage and break up the sausage meat. Clean the mushrooms, trimming the base of the stems and scraping off any soil with a small sharp knife. Try not to use water but, if absolutely necessary, clean carefully using a soft brush. Cut into slices. Heat the olive oil in a frying pan over a medium heat, add the garlic and cook for 1–2 minutes, until golden. Discard the garlic and add the sausage meat to the pan. Fry gently until golden, then add the prepared mushrooms and the thyme. Add salt to taste, taking into account the fact that Italian sausages are highly seasoned. Add pepper and cook for 8–10 minutes, stirring frequently to avoid sticking.

Meanwhile, bring a large pan of salted water to the boil over a high heat. Add the pumpkin gnocchi and cook until they rise to the surface. Remove with a slotted spoon and transfer to a serving bowl. Add the mushroom and sausage sauce, mix well and serve immediately.

Garden harvest

AUTUMN

Sorbetto d'anguria Watermelon sorbet

I never understood why people would carry home a heavy watermelon but I see now that its sweet,
fresh pulp lends itself to a multitude of uses, one of which is this delicate sorbet.

Serves 6

600g (1¼lb) watermelon,
deseeded and cut into pieces

150g (5oz/scant 1 cup) icing
(confectioners') sugar

mint leaves, to decorate

Mix the watermelon and icing (confectioners') sugar until the mixture becomes rather runny.

Pour into 6 freezer-proof sorbet moulds or glasses and freeze for 4 hours. Before serving,
soften in the refrigerator for 20 minutes. Serve decorated with mint leaves.

Sorbetto di fragole Strawberry sorbet

Strawberries picked at this time of year are incredibly sweet and fragrant; using them in a sorbet ensures they
retain all their flavour. Children will love you for this: it's the only dessert they'll eat apart from ice cream.

Serves 6

75ml (3fl oz/scant ⅓ cup)
water

60g (2½oz/generous ¼ cup)
caster (superfine) sugar

500g (1lb/generous 3¾ cups)
strawberries, hulled

75ml (3fl oz/scant ⅓ cup)
fresh orange juice, strained

Heat the water with the sugar in a small pan over a medium heat and bring to the boil.
Boil until it becomes syrupy, then leave to cool.

Whizz the strawberries briefly in a blender and mix with the cooled sugar syrup. Add the
orange juice and mix well. Pour into 6 freezer-proof sorbet moulds or glasses and freeze for
4 hours. Before serving, soften in the refrigerator for 20 minutes.

Ice pops Ice pops

I must say, it is very satisfying making ice cream at home.
All that churning is quite rewarding.

Serves 6

600ml (1 pint/2½ cups)
single (light) cream

3 tbsp caster (superfine)
sugar

140ml (scant ¼ pint/scant
⅔ cup) full-fat yogurt

100g (3½oz/¾ cup)
strawberries, hulled

juice of 1 unwaxed lemon,
strained

3 tbsp caster (superfine)
sugar

Pour the cream into a saucepan,
add the sugar and cook over a low
heat until the sugar has dissolved
completely. Remove from the heat and
leave to cool. Add the yogurt and pour
into an ice cream maker. Process for
40 minutes, until it has doubled
in quantity and is firm and creamy.

Meanwhile, wash and dry the
strawberries, cut in half and put in a
small pan with the lemon juice and
sugar. Cook over a medium heat for
5 minutes, then strain and return to
the heat to reduce. Pour into 6 small
freezer-proof glasses and leave to cool.

When the ice cream is ready, divide it
between the glasses. Push wooden
sticks into the ice cream and transfer
to the freezer for 4 hours.

To serve, remove from the freezer and
bring to room temperature.

Insalata d'anguria all'acqua di rose e erba Luigia
Watermelon salad with rosewater and lemon verbena

Watermelon pure and simple with just a nod to roses and the lemon. This is the most refined summer fruit salad that I have ever served. It is one of those simple recipes that your dinner guests will remember long afterwards. I have tried making it with other types of melon, but the result isn't so good.

Serves 6

1.5kg (3lb) watermelon

1 tbsp caster (superfine) sugar

4 tbsp rosewater

sprig of lemon verbena leaves

Cut the flesh away from the skin of the watermelon, then cut into even, medium-sized pieces, discarding the seeds as you go. Put on a deep plate to collect the juices. Transfer to a salad bowl and pour the juices over the top.

Dissolve the sugar in the rosewater and pour over the melon. Add the lemon verbena leaves and mix carefully into the salad. Cover with clingfilm (plastic wrap) and refrigerate for at least 1 hour. Serve cold.

Gelatina di pesche Peach jelly

I love jellies (jellos). They're not very Italian but they're a favourite of mine for experimentation. In this one, Prosecco, a symbol of the Veneto, goes really well with the taste and scent of ripe peaches – think Bellini cocktail. A fantastic alternative to classic ice creams and sorbets.

Serves 6

750ml (1¼ pints/3 cups) Prosecco

400g (13oz/generous 1¾ cups) caster (superfine) sugar

8 yellow peaches

20g (¾oz) leaf gelatine

Put the Prosecco in a saucepan with the sugar over a medium heat. Bring to the boil, stirring occasionally until the sugar has dissolved. Add the unpeeled peaches (the skin gives the jelly [jello] a lovely rosy colour), reduce the heat and cover the pan. Cook for 10–15 minutes, until the peaches are tender but have not lost their shape. Carefully transfer the peaches to a dish with a slotted spoon. Peel, cover with a quarter of the syrup and set aside.

Meanwhile, soak the gelatine leaves in cold water in a bowl for 4–5 minutes, remove from the bowl and squeeze out the excess water. Add the gelatine to the pan containing the remaining syrup and, still over a low heat, stir from time to time to dissolve. Leave to cool.

When the syrup is cold, pour into 6 jelly moulds (jello molds), previously rinsed in cold water. Cover with clingfilm (plastic wrap) and refrigerate for 4 hours, until the jellies (jellos) are set.

To serve, dip the moulds in hot water and use the point of a knife to free the jelly (jello) from the sides of the moulds. Turn out onto 6 serving plates. Serve with the peaches cut into quarters and the syrup.

Insalata di pollo con albicocche fresche e pinoli
Chicken salad with apricots and pine nuts

This recipe is for people who like strong flavours even though it is a light dish. I have to say that chicken breast cooked in a grape jelly is really appetizing and works well with the bitter sweetness of the fresh apricots. Turkey breast works well prepared this way, too.

Serves 6

2 tbsp extra virgin olive oil

2 tsp grape jelly (see below)

600g (1¼lb) chicken breasts, skin on

8 apricots

1 cucumber

3 tbsp rocket (arugula)

½ red onion, finely sliced

100g (3½oz/scant ⅔ cup) pine nuts, toasted

salt and freshly ground black pepper

for the dressing

40ml (scant 2fl oz/scant ¼ cup) best-quality extra virgin olive oil

1 tbsp freshly squeezed orange juice, strained

1 tsp Dijon mustard

Heat 1 tbsp of the olive oil in a frying pan over a low heat, add the grape jelly and cook for 2–3 minutes, until melted. Add the chicken breasts, increase the heat and cook for 6–8 minutes more (depending on the thickness) on each side, until the chicken is golden brown and cooked through. Add salt to taste, remove from the heat and leave to cool.

Wash and dry the apricots, then cut into quarters, discarding the stones (pits).

Peel the cucumber, cut in half lengthways, remove the seeds, then cut into thick slices. Place the slices in a bowl, sprinkle with salt and leave for 20 minutes.

Meanwhile, wash and pat the rocket (arugula) dry, discarding any tough stalks. Pat the cucumber slices dry. Cut the cooled chicken breasts into pieces and arrange on a serving dish. Add the apricots, cucumber, rocket (arugula), sliced onion and toasted pine nuts.

Make a dressing with the olive oil, orange juice and mustard. Pour over the salad and mix carefully. Add salt and pepper to taste and serve.

Gelatina di mosto
Grape jelly

This simple and delicious jelly is extremely versatile: it enhances a whole raft of dishes. I have used it with chicken breasts, which transforms it into something special. I also serve it with cheese, to bring out the flavour, and with goat's cheese tartlets (see p.106) – perfect for an outdoor snack.

Yield: about 750g (1½lb)

2kg (4lb) green or black grapes

625g (1¼lb/generous 2¾ cups) caster (superfine) sugar

1½ tsp dried pectin or 3 tsp agar-agar powder

Wash the grapes and separate them, then put them in a large bowl and press to obtain as much juice as possible. Add the sugar, mix well and leave overnight in a warm place. Transfer the pressed grapes and their juice to a saucepan and bring to the boil over a high heat. Reduce the heat and simmer for 40 minutes.

Remove from the heat and pass through a fine sieve, discarding the skins. Add the pectin or agar-agar powder and return to a low heat. Simmer for 5–7 minutes, then check for set by putting a teaspoonful on a cold plate. If the jelly is ready, the surface will be set and will crinkle when gently pushed with a finger.

Pour into jars while still hot. Eat straight away or sterilize (see p.148) and keep for up to 6 months.

Insalata di gamberi, zucchine e menta
Courgette, prawn and mint salad

This is *the* summer salad: there are no rules, there are no real quantities (but don't overdo the salt!). The only thing that remains consistent is to use really fresh seasonal produce. At this time of the year, salads made with fish and meat are for every occasion and everyone.

Serves 6

4 small courgettes (zucchini)

2 tbsp extra virgin olive oil, plus extra if needed

juice of ½ unwaxed lemon, strained

1 garlic clove, peeled and finely chopped

a few mint leaves, finely sliced

24 raw prawns (shrimp) cleaned and heads removed

3 small handfuls of baby salad leaves (salad greens)

salt and freshly ground black pepper

Wash and dry the courgettes (zucchini), then cut them lengthways into long, thin slices, using a mandolin. Put them on a plate and salt lightly.

Whisk the olive oil and lemon juice in a small bowl to make an emulsion, then add to the courgettes (zucchini) with the chopped garlic and the mint leaves. Leave to marinate in a cool place for at least 1 hour.

Meanwhile, bring a pan of lightly salted water to the boil. Add the prawns (shrimp) and cook for 1 minute, until they turn pink and are cooked through. Drain and leave to cool.

Wash and pat dry the baby salad leaves (salad greens). Shell the prawns (shrimp), mix with the marinated courgettes (zucchini) in a serving dish and add the salad leaves (salad greens). Add salt and pepper to taste and extra olive oil if necessary, then toss well. Serve immediately.

Pesce arrosto con limone confit e maionese all'estragone
Barbecued fish with lemon confit and tarragon mayonnaise

I only grill fish if I can use a big barbecue in the garden and no cheating! You can cook any fish this way as long as it is really fresh and hasn't been scaled. Always wait for the flames to die down to embers. The lemon confit is an extra bonus.

Serves 6

2 sea bass, about 1kg (2lb) each

2 tbsp mild extra virgin olive oil

salt and freshly ground black pepper

for the lemon confit

6 unwaxed lemons

500g (1lb/1⅔ cups) coarse salt

1 tbsp ground coriander

6 garlic cloves, peeled and finely chopped

sprig of rosemary

olive oil, to cover the lemon slices

for the tarragon mayonnaise

450ml (¾ pint/scant 2 cups) mayonnaise (preferably home-made)

3 sprigs of tarragon, finely chopped

Make the lemon confit a week in advance. To make, wash and dry the lemons thoroughly. They must be really dry to prevent fermentation. Cut the lemons into 3mm (⅛in) slices. Cover the base of a flat plate with a layer of coarse salt and arrange some of the lemon slices on top. Sprinkle with the coriander, the chopped garlic and some of the rosemary leaves. Add another layer of salt and repeat the process until all the lemon slices have been used up. Cover with clingfilm (plastic wrap) and refrigerate for 2 days.

After this time, layer the lemon slices in a large sterilized jar, pushing them down to avoid air pockets and covering the lemons with olive oil as you go. Continue until all the lemon slices have been layered, then top up with oil to ensure that they are all immersed in oil. Seal the jar and leave for 1 week.

For the mayonnaise, mix the mayonnaise with the finely chopped tarragon. Leave for at least 30 minutes so the mayonnaise absorbs the aromatic oils in the tarragon.

To cook the sea bass, light the charcoal for the barbecue.

Prepare the fish by cutting off the gills, then gutting and carefully rinsing the fish. Do not scale as the scales will protect the fish from the heat of the barbecue, thus avoiding singeing and helping to keep the flesh soft and moist.

Dry the fish carefully inside and out with paper towels, then score the flesh diagonally, twice on each side. Salt inside and out, brush with the olive oil, then sandwich the fish in a fish grill, laying a slice of lemon confit on each side of each fish.

When the flames have died down on the charcoal, put the fish on the barbecue about 10cm (4in) from the heat source. Cook for 5 minutes on each side, then cook for 15 minutes more, until cooked through, turning the fish occasionally and brushing them with oil from time to time. When the fish is cooked, place on a plate, add a little salt, pepper and a drizzle of olive oil, then serve with the tarragon mayonnaise and extra slices of lemon confit to garnish.

Mafaldine con scampi e zafferano
Malfaldine with scampi and saffron

Mafaldine pasta is soft in the middle and firm around the edges when cooked. I find it just right for this recipe:
it takes up the saffron perfectly and contrasts divinely with the texture of the scampi.

Serves 6

18 raw scampi tails, in the shell

1 garlic clove, peeled and finely chopped

zest of ½ lemon, finely grated

100ml (3½fl oz/scant ½ cup) extra virgin olive oil

pinch of saffron threads

480g (15oz) mafaldine pasta

handful of flat-leaf parsley

salt and freshly ground black pepper

Wash and peel the scampi tails, carefully removing the black filaments. Place in a bowl to marinate with the garlic and lemon zest. Moisten with plenty of olive oil, sprinkle with the saffron threads, cover with clingfilm (plastic wrap) and refrigerate for 2 hours.

Bring a large pan of salted water to the boil over a high heat, add the mafaldine, reduce the heat and cook for 10–13 minutes, until al dente. Remove the scampi and their marinade from the refrigerator, put in a large frying pan and add salt to taste. As soon as the pasta is ready, remove from the heat and drain. Add to the pan containing the scampi, toss together and place over a medium heat for 2 minutes, stirring gently and occasionally.

Meanwhile, chop the parsley finely. To serve, remove from the heat, add pepper to taste and a couple of pinches of parsley.

Polpettine di vitello con albicocche secche, mandorle tostate e timo con salsa estiva
Veal rissoles with apricots, almonds, thyme and summer sauce

As well as a perfect summer meal, these rissoles make brilliant canapés, served with a glass of cold Prosecco.
In the summer I prefer to use lighter meats and serve them as here with a sauce made with seasonal fruit.

Serves 6

400g (13oz) veal

100g (3½oz/⅔ cup) dried apricots

1 garlic clove

zest of ½ lemon

100g (3½oz/½ cup) cooked short-grain rice

1 egg, lightly beaten

100g (3½oz/scant ⅔ cup) almonds

olive oil or peanut oil, for deep-frying

200g (7oz/generous 2¾ cups) dry breadcrumbs

salt and black pepper

sprigs of thyme, to serve

for the summer sauce

2 peaches

5 cherry tomatoes

1 kiwi fruit

1 small red onion

1 chilli

1 tbsp ground cumin

1 tbsp caster (superfine) sugar

2 tbsp red wine vinegar

juice and grated zest of 1 lime

2 tbsp finely chopped mint leaves

2 tbsp extra virgin olive oil

To make the summer sauce, peel the peaches, remove the stones (pits) and dice the flesh. Halve the tomatoes, peel and roughly chop the kiwi, peel the red onion and chop finely, and deseed the chilli and chop finely. Mix these all together in a saucepan with the cumin, sugar, vinegar, lime juice and zest and mint. Add the olive oil and mix well. Put the pan over a low heat and cook for 15 minutes until you have a creamy sauce. Remove from the heat and set aside.

To make the rissoles, finely mince (grind) the veal, finely dice the dried apricots, peel and finely chop the garlic, and finely grate the lemon zest. Combine the veal with the rice, apricots, garlic, lemon zest and egg. Add salt and pepper to taste, mix well, then refrigerate for 30 minutes.

Blanch, peel, toast and roughly chop the almonds. Put the olive or peanut oil in a deep pan over a medium heat and heat to no more than 170°C (340°F).

Meanwhile, mix the breadcrumbs with the toasted almonds on a plate. Oil your hands with a few drops of oil and, taking a little of the meat mixture at a time, form into tiny round rissoles, not much bigger than a nutmeg. Roll the rissoles in the breadcrumb mixture, then deep-fry in the hot oil for 6 minutes, until golden brown. Remove with a slotted spoon and drain on paper towels. Serve warm with sprigs of thyme and with the summer sauce.

Crema fredda di melone al profumo di pepe e panelle
Pepper-scented chilled melon soup with chickpea panelle

There are many versions of this recipe, often accompanied by prosciutto crudo cut into slivers. I prefer to
enhance it with the fragrance and strong taste of black pepper and serve it with *panelle*, the fried street food
speciality from Palermo made with chickpea flour.

Serves 6

1 ripe, sweetly scented melon,
peeled and deseeded

100ml (3½ fl oz/scant ½ cup)
freshly squeezed orange
juice, strained

200g (7oz/generous ¾ cup)
fat-free Greek yogurt

salt

2 tbsp fruity extra virgin olive
oil

2 tsp coarsely ground black
pepper

for the panelle

200g (7oz/1⅓ cups) chickpea
flour

50ml (2fl oz/scant ¼ cup)
water

1 tbsp finely chopped flat-leaf
parsley

peanut or rapeseed oil, for
deep-frying

salt and freshly ground black
pepper

squeeze of lemon juice,
to serve

Start by making the *panelle*. Put the chickpea flour in a saucepan with the water, stir to
dissolve, then add salt to taste and the chopped parsley. Cook over a low heat, stirring
continuously.

When the mixture has reached the right consistency it will start coming away from the sides
of the pan. Immediately tip the mixture onto a marble or other cool surface and level it with
a spatula. Leave to cool, then cut into rectangles.

Put the peanut or rapeseed oil in a deep pan over a medium heat and heat to no more than
170°C (340°F). Deep-fry the *panelle* in the hot oil until crisp. Remove with a slotted spoon and
drain on paper towels.

To make the soup, cut the melon into pieces and process in a blender or electric juicer with
the orange juice. Add the yogurt and mix well. Add salt to taste and the olive oil and pepper.
Cover with clingfilm (plastic wrap) and refrigerate for at least 1 hour before serving.

When ready to serve, drizzle the *panelle* with lemon juice and serve with the soup.

Crema fredda di pomodori con basilico fritto e mozzarelline di bufala
Chilled tomato soup with fried basil and baby mozzarellas

This soup is made up of the key ingredients you expect to savour when dreaming about Italy: juicy sun-ripened
tomatoes, fresh, unmistakably milky-tasting mozzarella and intensely aromatic, slightly peppery basil picked at
just the right moment. Then there's the chilli. That's it done – just look at those colours ...

Serves 6

2 tbsp extra virgin olive oil,
plus extra to drizzle

1 garlic clove, finely chopped

1 red chilli, deseeded and
finely chopped

1 red onion, finely chopped

1.2 litres (2 pints/5 cups)
tomato passata

salt

18 basil leaves, to garnish

18 baby mozzarellas, to
garnish

Heat 1 tbsp of the olive oil in a saucepan over a medium heat, add the garlic and chilli and
fry, stirring occasionally, for 3 minutes – long enough for the oil to absorb the flavours of the
garlic and chilli but without burning them. Add the onion and cook for 5 minutes more,
until the onion is soft. Add the tomato passata and salt to taste. Stir well, reduce the heat and
cook for 15 minutes more.

Heat the remaining olive oil in a small pan over a low heat, add the basil leaves and fry until
crisp, taking care not to burn them. Remove the leaves from the pan, dab lightly with paper
towels, sprinkle with salt and set aside.

Remove the tomato soup from the heat, strain through a fine sieve, then transfer to
a soup tureen. Cover with clingfilm (plastic wrap), leave to cool, then refrigerate for at least
30 minutes before serving. Serve the soup garnished with the fried basil leaves, a few baby
mozzarellas and a good drizzle of olive oil.

Torta ai fichi con ricotta, mandorle e miele
Fig tart with ricotta, almonds and honey

I made this for the first time when friends came for dinner. After preparing it, I left it to cool in a corner of the kitchen. By 6.30 there was not a trace left of said pudding. Husband and son had to confess their guilty secret!

Serves 6–8

6 figs

2 tbsp caster (superfine) sugar

thyme leaves, to decorate

for the pastry (pie dough)

500g (1lb/3⅓cups) plain (all-purpose) flour, plus extra for dusting

pinch of salt

2 tbsp caster (superfine) sugar

2 eggs, lightly beaten

100g (3½oz/scant ½ cup) unsalted butter, softened

for the filling

500g (1lb/2½ cups) ricotta cheese

50g (2oz/generous ⅛ cup) clear honey

200g (7oz/scant 1⅔ cups) coarsely ground almonds

1 egg, lightly beaten

Make the pastry (pie dough). Sift the flour into a bowl with the salt and sugar, then add 10 tbsp warm water, the eggs and softened butter. Knead well until the mixture is smooth and elastic. Leave to rest for for 1 hour, then divide in 2 and leave the pieces on a flour-covered surface.

Grease a 50 x 70cm (20 x 28in) baking sheet. Carefully wash and dry the figs, then slice them thinly and set aside. Preheat the oven to 200°C (400°F/Gas 6).

Meanwhile, prepare the filling. In a bowl, mix together the ricotta, honey, almonds and egg until they form a smooth cream.

Stretch out the first piece of dough, lay it on the greased baking sheet and spread the ricotta mixture on top. Stretch out the second portion of dough and lay it on top. Press the edges of the pastry (pie dough) together firmly to seal. Arrange the thinly sliced figs on top and sprinkle with the sugar.

Place in the preheated oven and cook for about 40 minutes, checking after 30 minutes, until the pastry (pie dough) has puffed up and is browned. Remove from the oven and leave to cool slightly. Serve warm, sprinkled with thyme leaves.

Marmellata di fichi
Fig jam

Be sure not to overcook this jam as it dries out easily, and don't be taken aback if it is runny; once cooled, it becomes just the right consistency. As to the choice of cheese, I am a fundamentalist: Pecorino Sardo is *the* cheese to serve with fig jam.

Yield: 750g (1½lb)

1kg (2lb) figs

500g (1lb/generous 2¼ cups) caster (superfine) sugar

small piece of unwaxed lemon zest

mature (sharp) Pecorino Sardo cheese, to serve

Wash and dry the figs, then cut into quarters. Layer the figs with the sugar in a large saucepan and leave to rest for 2 hours so the figs absorb the sugar. Put the pan containing the figs over a medium heat, bring to the boil, then add the lemon zest. Reduce the heat and cook for 10 minutes, stirring frequently.

Remove the pan from the heat and pour the jam into jars. Eat straight away or sterilize (see p.148) and keep for up to 6 months.

Serve with mature (sharp) Pecorino Sardo cheese.

Fichi con nocciole e blu di capra
Figs with hazelnuts and blue goat's cheese

This salad falls within the category of 'poetic licence' food, which is why you can make it with your favourite cheese. I, however, recommend using a strong cheese to balance the sweetness of the ripe figs.

Serves 6

handful of wild rocket (arugula)

6 very ripe figs, washed, dried and halved

300g (10oz/generous 1 cup) blue goat's cheese, cut into small cubes

120g (scant 4oz/generous ¾ cup) shelled hazelnuts, roughly chopped

salt

extra virgin olive oil, to drizzle

Wash the rocket (arugula), discarding any tough pieces. To serve, arrange 2 fig halves on each plate with some cheese and rocket (arugula).

Scatter with some hazelnuts. Sprinkle with a pinch of salt and add a few drops of olive oil.

Panzanella di fichi secchi e non
Fresh and dried fig 'panzanella'

This is my take on the famous panzanella – the classic peasant salad of bread and tomatoes. The secret lies in the sweet and sour flavour underscored by the dried figs. I like to serve this fresh-tasting salad either as a small starter or as a main course, preferably after a plate of pasta.

Serves 6

400g (13oz) stale bread

4 ripe tomatoes

pinch of salt

1 red onion, thinly sliced

handful of mint leaves

6 very ripe fresh figs

4 dried figs, finely chopped

for the dressing

1 tbsp red wine vinegar

4 tbsp extra virgin olive oil

freshly ground black pepper

½ garlic clove, peeled and finely grated

Break the stale bread into bite-sized pieces, discarding any very hard pieces of crust. Set aside.

Wash the tomatoes, cut into slices, then put into a colander set over a dish to catch the juices. Sprinkle with the salt and set aside.

Put the onion in a salad bowl with the bread and a few mint leaves. Gently squeeze the tomatoes to extract any remaining juices and add the pulp to the bread and onion.

To make the dressing, put the collected tomato juices in a bowl and add the vinegar, olive oil, black pepper and garlic. Add more salt if necessary, then mix well and leave to stand for 10 minutes.

Meanwhile, wash and dry the fresh figs, then cut into quarters. Add these together with the chopped dried figs to the bread mixture. Pour over the dressing, toss carefully and leave to stand in a cool place for 20 minutes before serving.

Pizza con fichi, gorgonzola e rosmarino
Pizza with figs, gorgonzola and rosemary

This recipe uses a ready-made puff pastry base, creating a quasi-instant pizza. The important thing is the combination of figs and gorgonzola. If you prefer, you can just use gorgonzola, a mixture of gorgonzola and fresh mozzarella or simply mozzarella. The choice is yours.

Makes 1 pizza

500–750g (1lb–1½lb) ready-made puff pastry

150g (5oz) gorgonzola cheese, crumbled, or 100g (3½oz) gorgonzola and 50g (2oz) fresh fior di latte mozzarella, or 150g (5oz) fresh fior di latte mozzarella

2 figs, thinly sliced

sprig of rosemary

extra virgin olive oil, to drizzle

Preheat the oven to 180°C (350°F/Gas 4). Roll the pastry (pie dough) out to a circle roughly 30cm (12in) in diameter and place on a baking sheet. Spread the cheese on top of the pastry (pie dough) followed by the sliced figs. Add a few rosemary leaves and drizzle with a little olive oil.

Place in the preheated oven and bake for 20 minutes, until the cheese has completely melted and the pastry (pie dough) is golden and crisp.

Variation (using pizza dough)

This version uses traditional pizza dough, which naturally takes longer to make. But I can assure you it is a very satisfying way to spend an hour or so in the kitchen and making the dough is a wonderful skill to master. Use the topping combination described in the previous recipe.

15g (½oz) fresh brewer's yeast

250ml (8fl oz/1 cup) warm water

pinch of caster (superfine) sugar

500g (1lb/3⅓ cups) 00 flour, plus extra for dusting

2 tbsp extra virgin olive oil

pinch of salt

100g (3½oz) fresh fior di latte mozzarella (optional)

Preheat the oven to 220C° (425°F/Gas 7). Dissolve the yeast in the water and add the sugar. Put the flour in a large bowl, make a well in the centre and add the water and yeast mixture. Mix well, then add the olive oil and salt. Knead together thoroughly until the dough is soft and springy.

Cover with a clean cloth and leave to prove for 45 minutes to 1 hour, until the dough has doubled in size. Roll out the dough on a floured surface to make a circle roughly 30cm (12in) in diameter and place on a baking sheet. Top with the ingredients as described above. You may add 100g (3½oz) *fior di latte* mozzarella if you wish.

Bake in the preheated oven for 20 minutes, until the cheese has completely melted and the dough is golden and crusty.

Think of temptation and what immediately comes to mind is

figs. For me, no other fruit better fits the definition of temptation, in all probability because of that soft, sugary pulp, with its beautiful rosy colour, which simply melts in your mouth. Every year, when the trees in my garden fill with ripe figs, I conduct personal tasting sessions. I take my time, lingering over each plant and yet, when the round is complete, I find myself beginning all over again! Figs on their own, figs with cheese, figs in salad, figs on a tart or a pizza – these moments of sublime pleasure are always assured. At home the fig harvest always surprises us with its size and so every year part of it, together perhaps with some barely toasted almonds and the zest of a lemon, is made into splendid jam. Figs should be soft but not mushy and free from bruises or cuts on the skin. Whether picked or freshly bought, they should be arranged on a plate and put in the refrigerator, where they will keep for up to three days. They should be taken out some time before they are to be eaten, as it is at room temperature that their richly ripe flavour may be most fully appreciated.

Pane casereccio con fichi confit, formaggio fresco di capra e timo
Crusty bread with bottled figs, soft goat's cheese and thyme

Considering I like to keep things simple, this dish is bordering on the luxurious: the smell of fresh bread, the taste of goat's milk sweetened by this extraordinarily juicy fruit and the strong scent of thyme. Good to eat at the end of a meal, at the beginning or even as a mid-morning snack.

Serves 6

150g (5oz/⅓ cup) soft goat's cheese

6 slices of ciabatta or a similar crusty bread

extra virgin olive oil, to drizzle

salt and freshly ground black pepper

a few thyme leaves, to garnish

for the bottled figs

2 litres (3½ pints/8½ cups) water

800g (1½lb/scant 3⅔ cups) caster (superfine) sugar

1 vanilla pod (bean), slit lengthways

12 figs

To make the bottled figs, put the water and sugar in a pan over a medium heat, bring to the boil and boil for 10 minutes. Take the pan off the heat, add the vanilla pod (bean) and leave to cool.

Meanwhile, carefully wash and dry the figs and put them in a large glass jar. When the syrup has cooled, pour it over the figs, adding the vanilla pod (bean). Seal the jar and refrigerate for at least 3 hours.

To serve, spread a little goat's cheese on each slice of bread, add a pinch of salt and pepper and a drizzle of olive oil. Remove the figs from the jar, squeeze them gently, cut in half and arrange on top of the cheese. Garnish with a few thyme leaves.

Figs

Torta di albicocche
Apricot tart

The puddings I enjoy most are the simple ones. I don't have a sweet tooth, alas, but a tart made with summer fruits is a good reason to try and develop one. You can add 70g (scant 3oz/½ cup) of roughly chopped almonds to the mixture, to make this pudding even more irresistible.

Serves 6

1kg (2lb) apricots, plus 2 extra, to decorate

150g (5oz/scant ⅔ cup) butter, plus extra for greasing

100g (3½oz/½ cup) caster (superfine) sugar, plus extra for sprinkling

2 eggs

200g (7oz/1⅓ cups) 00 flour, sifted

1 sachet of dried yeast

sprig of mint, to decorate

Preheat the oven to 180°C (350°F/Gas 4). Wash and dry the apricots, then slice, removing the stones (pits). Set 2 apricots aside for the decoration.

Grease the bottom of a 25cm (10in) flan tin (tart pan) and sprinkle with sugar. Place the prepared apricots in the tin (pan) so they completely cover the base.

Beat the butter and sugar together in a bowl until soft and fluffy. Continuing to beat, add the eggs, flour and yeast.

Pour the mixture over the apricots and level it off using a spatula. Place in the preheated oven and cook for about 40–50 minutes, until the top is cooked through.

Remove from the oven and leave to cool, Turn upside down onto a dish. Serve, decorated with the 2 reserved apricots and the sprig of mint.

Cartoccio di verdure dell'orto al forno
Roast vegetable packet

This recipe sings the praises of my kitchen garden; before it gets hot, I gather the pick of the crop. I just add some respect, a herb or two and a splash of good oil, then I let the vegetables do the rest. You can make this with any vegetables as long as they are morning fresh.

Serves 6–8

1 each red and yellow pepper (bell pepper)

3 spring onions (scallions)

2 small potatoes

1 carrot

1 aubergine (eggplant)

2 leeks

2 red onions, peeled

1 each hot green and red chilli pepper

2 courgettes (zucchini)

a few small sprigs of thyme, oregano and marjoram

large pinch of coarse salt

2 tbsp extra virgin olive oil

Preheat the oven to 180°C (350°F/Gas 4). Cut the peppers in half and remove the seeds. Peel the spring onions (scallions), making sure you keep some of the green parts. Cut the potatoes in half without peeling. Wash the carrot and make an incision along its length without cutting it in half. Cut the aubergine (eggplant) in half.

Clean the leeks, discarding the tough outer bits, then cut into lengths. Cut the onions in half. Discard the seeds of the chilli peppers; wear gloves to prevent skin rashes. Trim the courgettes (zucchini) and wash and dry the herbs.

Run a large sheet of baking parchment (parchment paper) under cold running water, squeeze it out and lay it in the bottom of a roasting tin (pan). Arrange the vegetables on top of the paper, then add 3–4 tbsp water, the salt, herbs and olive oil. Cover with a second sheet of parchment, then place in the preheated oven and cook for 15 minutes. Remove the top sheet of parchment and continue to cook for 10 minutes more, until the vegetables start to turn golden brown but still have some bite. Serve warm as a side dish.

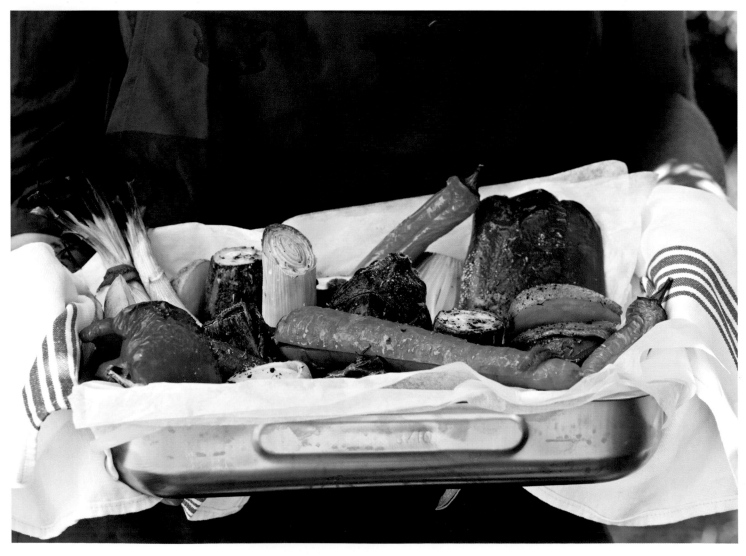

Boulettes di agnello con salsa allo jogurt e erba cipollina
Lamb rissoles with yogurt and chive sauce

This is a clever way of serving a meat dish in summer. The herbs give freshness to the lamb and the warm rissoles are really tasty with the yogurt sauce. I can assure you that these skewered lamb rissoles are perfectly in tune with our appetites and the heat of summer.

Serves 6

1kg (2lb) lean lamb, off the bone

1 egg white

salt and freshly ground black pepper

sprig of mint

sprig of coriander (cilantro)

for the yogurt sauce

250g (8oz/1 cup) plain yogurt

1 tbsp sour cream

1½ garlic cloves, peeled and crushed

6–8 chives, finely snipped

1 tsp extra virgin olive oil

salt and freshly ground black pepper

for the garnish

1 tbsp extra virgin olive oil

12 spring onions (scallions), trimmed

Preheat the oven to 180°C (350°F/Gas 4). Cut the lamb into small cubes and put in a food processor with the egg white, salt, pepper, mint and coriander (cilantro). Whizz briefly so it is not too finely ground.

Roll the mixture between your hands to make 18 small, evenly sized rissoles. Put in a shallow roasting dish, place in the preheated oven and cook for 15–20 minutes, checking for doneness after 15 minutes. Remove from the oven and leave to cool.

Meanwhile, make the yogurt sauce and prepare the garnish. Mix together the yogurt, sour cream, garlic, chives and olive oil in a bowl. Add salt and pepper to taste.

Heat the olive oil in a frying pan over a medium heat, add the spring onions (scallions) and cook for 5–7 minutes, until lightly browned.

To serve, thread the rissoles onto skewers, alternating them with the spring onions (scallions). Serve warm or cold with the yogurt sauce.

Crema di peperoni ghiacciata con cheese straws
Cream of pepper soup with cheese straws

I first served this deliciously refreshing cold soup for a summer lunch. It was so satisfying to see my son
Nicolò and his friends tuck into a vegetable soup with such gusto and munching on the cheese straws.
Try using cumin instead of the sesame seeds. They are really tasty too.

Serves 6

6 plump red peppers (bell peppers)

3 tbsp extra virgin olive oil

2 garlic cloves, peeled

2 sprigs of thyme

4 pinches of caster (superfine) sugar

salt and freshly ground black pepper

for the cheese straws (makes 18)

70g (scant 3oz/generous ¼ cup) unsalted butter, softened

140g (scant 5oz/scant 1 cup) plain (all-purpose) white flour

pinch of salt

70g (scant 3oz/generous ½ cup) grated mature (sharp) Cheddar cheese

2 eggs

1 tbsp Dijon mustard

2 tbsp sesame seeds

Preheat the grill (broiler) to maximum temperature. Put the peppers on the preheated grill (broiler) and grill for 10 minutes, until the skin blisters. Turn the peppers over and cook for 8 minutes more. Place in a bowl and cover with clingfilm (plastic wrap). Leave to rest for 15 minutes, then peel the skin away and slice the flesh, taking care to remove the seeds. Set aside.

Heat the olive oil in a non-stick pan over a medium heat, add the garlic and thyme and cook for 3 minutes, until the garlic starts to turn golden brown. Add the sliced peppers, mix well and cook for 5 minutes more, adding salt, pepper and sugar to taste. Remove from the heat and whizz to a smooth cream in a blender. Refrigerate for at least 1 hour.

Meanwhile, make the cheese straws. Rub the butter into the flour using the fingertips until it resembles crumbs, then add the salt and grated cheese. In another bowl, beat together the eggs and mustard, then add about half to the flour and butter mixture. Mix thoroughly to make a smooth dough, then leave to rest for 10 minutes.

Preheat the oven to 180°C (350°F/Gas 4) and line a baking sheet with baking parchment (parchment paper).

Toast the sesame seeds in a dry frying pan over a medium heat, stirring frequently to ensure they do not burn. Remove from the heat to cool, then mix into the chilled dough.

Roll the dough out to about ½cm (¼in) thick, then cut into 18 strips. Place on the baking sheet, brush with the leftover beaten egg and bake in the preheated oven for 12 minutes.

Serve the cream of pepper soup ice cold, accompanied by the cheese straws.

Millefoglie di melanzana al pesto di pomodoro
Millefeuille of aubergine, mozzarella and sundried tomato

For a lighter version of this recipe, make it with griddled aubergines (eggplants). There is no need to salt the aubergines (eggplants) if you make it this way; simply cut in slices, brush lightly with olive oil and cook on a ridged griddle for 3 minutes on each side. Salt lightly, then proceed as per the recipe.

Serves 6

3 large aubergines (eggplants)

1 tbsp salted capers

100ml (3½fl oz/scant ½ cup) extra virgin olive oil, plus extra to drizzle

120g (scant 4oz/generous ¾ cup) sundried tomatoes in oil, drained

30g (1oz/¼ cup) taggiasca olives, stones (pits) removed

2 anchovy fillets in oil, drained

1 garlic clove, peeled

1 tbsp dried oregano

pinch of chilli powder

1 mozzarella di bufala, roughly sliced

basil leaves, to garnish

Cut the aubergines (eggplants) into about 18 thin rounds, sprinkle with salt and leave to drain for 30 minutes. Rinse the capers in cold water to remove the salt, squeeze and dry well with paper towels. Dry the aubergines (eggplants) with paper towels.

Heat 1 tbsp of the olive oil in a non-stick frying pan over a medium heat and fry the aubergine (eggplant) on both sides until golden.

Chop together the sundried tomatoes, capers, olives, anchovy fillets and garlic, then add the dried oregano, chilli powder and the remaining olive oil.

Layer the sliced aubergine (eggplant), the sundried tomato mixture and the mozzarella slices on 6 serving plates. Drizzle with olive oil and serve, garnished with a few basil leaves.

Dentice con verdure e profumi dell'orto
Snapper and vegetables with the scent of the kitchen garden

It is easy to cook a big fish. The rules are: the fish must be really fresh and the cooking times adhered to so that the fish neither dries out nor is undercooked. When in doubt it is always better to give it a minute or so less rather than more.

Serves 6

600g (1¼lb) vine tomatoes

2 tbsp extra virgin olive oil, plus extra to drizzle

3 garlic cloves, peeled

1 potato, peeled and cut into small cubes

3 spring onions (scallions), peeled, green part discarded and cut in half

1 x 1.5kg (3lb) red snapper

½ tbsp coarse salt

100g (3½oz/generous ¾ cup) taggiasca olives, stones (pits) removed

1 sprig of wild fennel, plus extra to garnish

1 piece of lemon zest

Bring a pan of salted water to the boil over a high heat, then reduce the heat, immerse the tomatoes and cook for 4–5 minutes. Drain and skin. Discard the seeds and cut into small pieces.

Heat the olive oil in a large fish kettle over a medium heat, add the garlic and fry for 1 minute, stirring frequently to ensure it does not burn. Add the tomatoes, potato and spring onion (scallion) and cook for 2–3 minutes, stirring occasionally until the vegetables start to soften.

Put the snapper in the pan and add 3 ladles of water and the salt. Cover the pan and cook for 10 minutes more. Add the olives, fennel and lemon zest and cook for 15–20 minutes more, until the fish is cooked through.

Carefully remove the cooked snapper from the fish kettle. Serve with the vegetables, cooking juices and a drizzle of olive oil, then garnish with wild fennel.

E very image is a reflection of a piece of work which, in turn, stems from a project. In this case, the project revolved entirely around my kitchen garden: I saw that it had the potential to be much more than just a kitchen garden. Some years ago I was telling my husband, Valerio, how much I would like to be able to organize dinners with friends there. We fantasized together about the possible options and I, being the less technically minded of the two, was already imagining the effect of candles among the vegetables and flowers. As it turned out, all I had to do was to go away for a few days. On my return I found the object of my dreams – amid aubergines, fennel and basil, a small platform, made of antique paving stones, had appeared. In Valerio's opinion the platform was large enough to accommodate four; in mine it would take eight close friends. This small space immediately became my favourite setting for summer dinners – the ideal place for savouring garden produce which, before passing through my hands, had already enjoyed the greater benefits brought to it by the sun. Just an aside: I am firmly of the opinion that at the table, humankind should gather closely together – spatially as well as metaphorically speaking!

Insalata di pomodori Tomato salad

I kept asking myself if this recipe was bordering on the banal but I realized that one of the basics of Italian food is superb produce. To avoid disappointment, only make this simple dish in season with sun-ripened tomatoes, dressed with the very best extra virgin olive oil and a pinch of salt. You can use any tomatoes, as long as you include at least three different varieties.

Serves 6

5 basil leaves

500g (1lb) mixed variety tomatoes (such as Costoluto, Cuore di Bue, Yellow Pear, Locarno, Perino, Nero and Zebrino)

4 tbsp fragrant extra virgin olive oil

2 pinches of salt

Wash and dry the basil leaves. Wash the tomatoes and cut into wedges. Put the tomatoes in a serving dish with the olive oil, salt and basil leaves.

Leave in a cool place for 10 minutes before serving.

Kitchen garden

SUMMER

Crème brûlée alla rosa
Rose crème brûlée

Take my advice – make a few extra portions of this. My guests are never happy with just one waltz! Sprinkle the custards with sugar just before serving and if, by chance, your guests are less greedy than mine, cover the leftovers with clingfilm (plastic wrap) and they will keep in the refrigerator for two days.

Serves 6

1 Bourbon vanilla pod (bean)

500ml (17fl oz/2 cups) single (light) cream

½ tsp rose essential oil for human consumption

5 egg yolks

100g (3½oz/½ cup) caster (superfine) sugar

6–8 tbsp granulated pure cane sugar

12 fresh rose petals, to decorate

Preheat the oven to 130°C (250°F/Gas ½). Cut the vanilla pod (bean) open and use the tip of a knife to scrape out the seeds. Put the seeds and the cream in a small pan, place over a medium heat and bring to the boil, stirring continuously. Remove from the heat, leave to cool for 10 minutes, then add the rose essential oil. Meanwhile, beat the egg yolks and caster (superfine) sugar together in a large bowl until well blended. Pour the cream over the sugar and egg yolk mixture and mix well.

Prepare 6 small ovenproof ramekins by wetting them, then pour in the cream and egg yolk mixture. Put the ramekins in a roasting dish two-thirds filled with water, then place in the preheated oven and cook for 50 minutes to 1 hour. Check them from time to time. They are ready when the surface is firm and golden brown.

Remove from the oven and leave to cool, then cover the surface with the cane sugar and caramelize using a blowtorch or by placing under the grill (broiler) for 1–2 minutes. To serve, decorate with rose petals.

Torta dolce rosa ai petali glassati e angelica
Sweet rose torta with crystallized petals and angelica

This simple sponge started with a beautiful piece of angelica bought in Paris. Once I got it home I knew it had to be made into something really lovely – a pink iced cake shaped like a rose and decorated with angelica, raspberries and sugared rose petals ... et voilà!

Serves 6

300g (10oz/2 cups) 00 flour, sifted

10 eggs, separated

200g (7oz/scant 1 cup) caster (superfine) sugar

2 tbsp lemon juice

for the crystallized rose petals

1 egg white

15–20 fresh rose petals

50g (2oz/scant ⅓ cup) icing (confectioners') sugar, sifted

for the glacé icing (frosting)

220g (7½oz/generous 1⅓ cups) icing (confectioners') sugar, sifted

2–3 tbsp warm water

a few drops of rose pink food colouring

to decorate

3 stems of candied angelica

handful of raspberries

Prepare the crystallized rose petals. Place the egg white in a bowl and whisk lightly. Quickly immerse the petals one by one in the egg white, shake off any excess, then arrange on a wire rack. Dust with the sifted icing (confectioners') sugar and leave until completely dry.

Preheat the oven to 200°C (400°F/Gas 6).

Put the 10 egg yolks and the sugar in a large bowl and beat together until thick and creamy. Set aside.

Put the 10 egg whites in a second bowl and whisk to form stiff peaks.

Add the sifted flour to the egg yolk and sugar mixture, then fold in the beaten egg whites and the lemon juice. Pour the mixture into a 23cm (9in) diameter rose-shaped silicone cake mould. Place in the preheated oven and cook for 30 minutes, taking care not to open the oven during this time. When the sponge has risen and is springy to the touch, remove from the oven and leave to cool in the tin (pan).

Meanwhile, make the glacé icing (frosting). Put the icing (confectioners') sugar in a bowl and add 2 tbsp of the water. Mix together carefully with a wooden spoon until smooth and of a good, thick coating consistency. It may be necessary to add more water; if so, add a few drops at a time. Beat in enough rose pink food colouring to create the shade required.

Turn out the sponge and put on a serving plate. Cover with the glacé icing (frosting) and when this has set, decorate with the candied angelica, crystallized rose petals and a few raspberries.

Salmone e zucchine al profumo di origano fresco e olio alla rosa, sale affumicato e

Salmon and courgettes with oregano, rose oil and smoked salt

This play on tastes works well, is attractive and well balanced. The salmon is a fish that lends itself perfectly to strong flavours without the risk of losing its personality, and this dish is the proof of just that. It is fragrant and aromatic and a great alternative to more classic fish dishes. A simple yet impressive dish.

Serves 6

1kg (2lb) salmon

200ml (7fl oz/generous ¾ cup) good-quality extra virgin olive oil, plus 1 tbsp

½ tsp rose essential oil for human consumption

100g (3½oz/⅔ cup) pistachio nuts, shelled

4 courgettes (zucchini)

smoked salt

salt and freshly ground black pepper

oregano leaves, to garnish

Wash the salmon, remove the skin, cut it into slices and then into medium-sized cubes.

Mix the olive oil with the rose essential oil in a bowl, then pour the resulting marinade over the salmon cubes. Cover with clingfilm (plastic wrap) and refrigerate for 15 minutes.

Roughly grind the pistachio nuts in a mortar and pestle. Heat a dry frying pan over a medium heat, add the ground pistachio nuts and toast for 1 minute, stirring frequently to ensure they do not burn. Remove from the heat and leave to cool.

Wash and dry the courgettes (zucchini), then cut into small cubes. Heat the remaining 1 tbsp olive oil in a non-stick frying pan over a medium heat, then add the courgettes (zucchini) and fry for 6–7 minutes, until crisp and golden, stirring frequently to ensure they do not burn. Add salt to taste and set aside.

Heat a clean non-stick pan over a low heat, add the marinated salmon with its marinade and cook for 2 minutes, stirring frequently. The salmon should be a little pink in the middle. Add the fried courgettes (zucchini), season to taste with the smoked salt and black pepper and mix well.

To serve, divide the salmon and courgette (zucchini) mixture between 6 plates, sprinkle with the toasted pistachio nuts and garnish with a few oregano leaves.

Piccole tartare di tonno con wasabi alla mela e julienne di rose
Tuna tartares with apple-flavoured wasabi and rose julienne

Tuna fish tartare is already well known and loved but I think that this version, with its rose petals, is incredible. It is wonderful to choose your petals when the roses are in season and add them to a dish. The note of wasabi sweetened with apple makes this recipe even more intriguing. PICTURED ON PAGE 40

Serves 6

600g (1¼lb) piece of very fresh, best-quality tuna

160g (5½oz/½ cup) organic apple purée

1½ tsp wasabi paste

pinch of salt

good-quality extra virgin olive oil, to drizzle

50g (2oz/scant ⅓ cup) pine nuts

fresh rose petals, cut into fine julienne strips, to garnish

Wash the tuna, remove the skin, cut it into slices and then into medium-sized cubes.

In a small bowl, mix together the apple purée, wasabi, salt and a drizzle of olive oil. Set aside.

Put the cubed tuna in a bowl, add the apple and wasabi mixture, setting aside 6 tsp of the mixture, and mix well. Add the pine nuts, mix again, then leave to stand for 10 minutes.

Place 6 tian rings on plates and fill with the tuna fish mixture, pressing down gently.

Before serving, carefully remove the tian rings, place 1 tsp apple and wasabi mixture on top of each tuna tartare and decorate with the julienned rose petals. Add a final drizzle of olive oil to each plate.

Gazpacho d'anguria al profumo di rosa e menta
Rose and mint-scented watermelon gazpacho

This is an interesting take on the classic Andalusia gazpacho. The presence of the roses is very subtle and leaves room for the lively fresh notes of the gazpacho. Serve with lightly toasted crostini or with cucumber sticks marinated in a pinch or two of salt for 15 minutes. PICTURED ON PAGE 41

Serves 6

500g (1lb) firm tomatoes

½ red pepper (bell pepper), pith removed, deseeded and roughly chopped

1 cucumber, peeled, deseeded and roughly chopped

500g (1lb) watermelon, peeled, sliced and deseeded

1 red onion, roughly chopped

1 garlic clove, chopped

3 pinches of salt

2 tbsp extra virgin olive oil

3 tbsp sherry vinegar

handful of mint leaves

30ml (2 tbsp) rosewater

to garnish
mint leaves

½ red onion, thinly sliced

fresh rose petals (optional)

Immerse the tomatoes briefly in plenty of boiling water, then remove, hold under cold water, then dry with paper towels. Skin the tomatoes, cut them in half and remove the seeds, then put in a blender.

Add the red pepper, whizz briefly, then add the cucumber and whizz again briefly. Add the watermelon, red onion, garlic, salt and oil. Whizz everything up together, then add the sherry vinegar a little at a time, whizzing again between additions.

Refrigerate the gazpacho for at least 1–2 hours.

Cut the mint leaves into fine julienne strips and add to the gazpacho with the rosewater.

To serve, stir well, divide between the soup bowls, then garnish with a few whole mint leaves, the thinly sliced red onion and the rose petals, if desired.

When a rose blooms, a little miracle happens in the kitchen. Our senses leap into action like the well-tuned instruments of an orchestra. This flower requires special attention: we should be in no hurry to uncover the firm rosebud enshrined in its crown of petals, nor hasten to surrender to its charm and succumb to its beauty. The choice of roses as an ingredient is a truly personal one. A particular mood or occasion could perfectly well be my excuse for turning to this magnificent flower. In general, it may be said that any roses with scented flowers can be used for cooking, provided that they have not been treated with chemicals. We therefore think it best to choose organic roses or those picked straight from our garden in May. Another important factor to take into consideration is the scent of the rose; this probably constitutes the most decisive of its sensorial characteristics, the one most capable of swiftly evoking sensations in us that are totally divorced from reason. That is why the rose proves itself a true and worthy ingredient and one that, thanks to its smell and taste, is well equipped to enhance and prolong the pleasures of the table.

Crudo di branzino con gamberi rossi marinati in vinaigrette di frutto della passione
Crudo of sea bass and prawns in a passion-fruit vinaigrette

Here I have used passion fruit flesh to give acidity to the marinade. It is tempered by adding rosewater, which gives the marinade an even more delicate taste. This marinade works perfectly for fish such as sea bass and prawns (shrimp). However, you could consider it for any type of crudo – swordfish or salmon, for example.

Serves 6

36 raw prawns (shrimp), in the shell

1 x 1.2kg (2½lb) sea bass, cleaned and thinly filleted

for the marinade
6 passion fruits
2 tbsp rosewater
2 pinches of salt
1 tsp caster (superfine) sugar
2 tbsp extra virgin olive oil

to garnish
10–12 fresh rose petals
8–10 pink peppercorns
fennel fronds, chopped
lemon verbena leaves, chopped
mint leaves, chopped

Make the marinade by cutting the passion fruit in half and, using a teaspoon, scoop the flesh and seeds into a bowl. Add the rosewater, salt, sugar and the olive oil. Whisk together and refrigerate for 10 minutes.

Meanwhile, wash and dry the prawns (shrimp). Remove the heads and peel away the shells. Remove any black filaments with tweezers.

Arrange the sea bass fillets and the prawns (shrimp) on a serving platter. Pour over half the marinade, cover with clingfilm (plastic wrap) and refrigerate for 15 minutes.

Remove from the refrigerator and garnish with rose petals, a few pink peppercorns, chopped fennel fronds, lemon verbena leaves and mint leaves. Serve with the remaining marinade on the side.

Lunch
with roses

Torta agli asparagi
Asparagus tart

I believe that asparagus is much more versatile than most people think. When white asparagus is cooked with honey, as here, it takes on a really subtle flavour with just a note of sweetness. However, in the case of this recipe, I think the secret lies in that final sprinkling of nutmeg that brings out the true flavour.

Serves 6

200g (7oz) white asparagus tips, cut in half lengthways

2 tbsp clear honey

1 tbsp extra virgin olive oil

90ml (scant 3½fl oz/ generous ⅓ cup) milk

1 vanilla pod (bean), sliced open lengthways

3 large eggs

130g (4oz/generous ½ cup) caster (superfine) sugar, plus extra for sprinkling

3 egg yolks

ground nutmeg, for sprinkling

dried butter (lima) beans, for blind baking

for the pastry (pie dough)

2 tbsp caster (superfine) sugar

240g (scant 8oz/scant 1⅔ cups) plain (all-purpose) white flour, sifted

120g (scant 4oz/½ cup) unsalted butter, diced, plus extra for greasing

3 tbsp cold water

1 egg white, lightly beaten

Make the pastry (pie dough). Mix the sugar with the sifted flour, add the butter and mix to a smooth, soft dough with the cold water. Wrap in clingfilm (plastic wrap) and leave to rest in the refrigerator for 30 minutes.

Meanwhile, line a baking sheet with baking parchment (parchment paper) and grease a 25cm (10in) tart tin (pan) ring with a removable base.

Remove the pastry (pie dough) from the refrigerator and roll it out directly onto the lined baking sheet to a thickness of 3mm (⅛in). Put the tart ring on the pastry (pie dough) and cut round it.

Leave the tart ring in place, gather up the remaining pastry (pie dough), roll it out to make a long strip and use to line the inside of the tart ring. Press the strip firmly to the ring.

Cover with clingfilm (plastic wrap) and leave to rest in a cool place for 15 minutes, preferably in the refrigerator.

Preheat the oven to 190°C (375°F/Gas 5).

Remove the tart from the refrigerator, line the base with baking parchment (parchment paper) and fill with dried butter (lima) beans. Place in the preheated oven and cook for 10 minutes. Remove from the oven and set aside.

Remove from the oven, reduce the heat to 150°C (300°F/Gas 2), discard the paper and beans, paint the base of the tart with the lightly beaten egg white, then return to the oven for 7–8 minutes more, until firm.

Meanwhile, wash and dry the asparagus tips.

Heat the honey and olive oil in a frying pan over a low heat. As soon as they start to caramelize, add the asparagus tips and fry gently for 4–5 minutes, stirring gently. Remove from the heat and set aside.

Heat the milk gently in a saucepan with the vanilla pod (bean) for 10 minutes without boiling. Remove from the heat, leave to infuse for 10 minutes more, then discard the vanilla pod (bean).

Beat the whole eggs with the sugar in a bowl, then add the egg yolks and stir well with a wooden spoon until smooth.

Put the saucepan of infused milk over a very low heat and gradually add the egg and sugar mixture, stirring all the time until the mixture thickens. Take care not to boil as the eggs will curdle. As soon as the mixture coats the back of the spoon, add the reserved asparagus and stir gently.

Pour the mixture into the tart and sprinkle with sugar and nutmeg. Place in the oven and bake for 1½ hours, until the mixture is set firm. Remove from the oven, leave to cool, then serve.

Triglie al forno con asparagi arrosto
Baked red mullet with roast asparagus

Here, where the red mullet comes straight from the sea, the experts cook it without gutting it first, which seems to enhance the delicate flavour of the flesh. This is a simple yet refined dish that you enjoy just by looking at it: the red of the fish and the green and white of the asparagus prepare you for a feast of flavours.

Serves 6

1 tbsp extra virgin olive oil

2 garlic cloves, peeled and halved

6 black peppercorns

2 sprigs of oregano

3 pieces orange zest

300g (10oz) green asparagus

300g (10oz) white asparagus

6 red mullet or other small, tasty fish, about 200g (7oz) each

salt and freshly ground black pepper

The day before, whisk together the olive oil, garlic cloves, peppercorns, oregano and orange zest to make an emulsion. The next day, preheat the oven to 180°C (350°F/Gas 4). Wash all the asparagus, then bend each spear of the green asparagus. The spear should snap easily at the point where the woody part begins. Discard the tough, woody base. Prepare the white asparagus by cutting away any tough bits at the base of the spears, then using a potato peeler to remove any stringy outer parts. Bring a pan of salted water to the boil over a high heat, add the trimmed asparagus, reduce the heat and simmer for 3 minutes. Drain and pat dry.

Meanwhile, prepare the red mullet. Cut off the fins, then scale and gut the fish. Rinse in cold running water, then dry carefully. Put the fish in a roasting tin (pan) with the garlic, oregano, orange zest and the emulsion, keeping back a little of its oil for later use. Season with salt and pepper to taste. Place the tin (pan) in the preheated oven and roast for 15 minutes.

While the fish is in the oven, pour the reserved oil into a frying pan over a medium heat, add the asparagus spears and fry for 5 minutes, turning occasionally, until golden brown. Remove the asparagus from the pan and add to the roasting tin (pan) with the red mullet. Return to the oven and bake for 5 minutes more, until cooked through.

Remove from the oven and discard the garlic, oregano and orange zest. Serve immediately.

Tagliatelle con asparagi, mandorle e menta
Tagliatelle with asparagus, almonds and mint

There are many different ways of serving pasta and asparagus but this is by far my favourite. In the cookery book classics, asparagus is always accompanied by or rather, accompanies scampi, but I think the crunchiness of the toasted almonds and the freshness of the mint perfectly enhance the delicate taste of the asparagus.

Serves 6

750g (1½lb) green asparagus

18 tips of white asparagus

90g (3½oz/generous ½ cup) almonds, blanched and peeled

10 mint leaves

2 tbsp extra virgin olive oil, plus extra to drizzle

1 garlic clove, peeled

480g (15oz) egg tagliatelle

salt and freshly ground black pepper

3 tbsp grated Pecorino cheese, to serve

Wash the green asparagus, then bend each spear. The spear should snap easily at the point where the woody part begins. Discard the tough, woody base.

Cut the green asparagus into 5cm (2in) pieces. Bring a pan of salted water to the boil over a high heat, add the pieces of stem and the white asparagus and cook for 8 minutes. Drain and dry well.

Meanwhile, heat a dry frying pan over a medium heat, add the almonds and toast until just golden, then remove and chop roughly.

Heat the olive oil in a frying pan over a medium heat, add the garlic clove and discard it as soon as it starts to turn golden brown. Add all the asparagus and fry for 3 minutes, taking care not to break the tips. Shake the pan gently to stop them sticking.

Remove from the heat and add the mint leaves, almonds and seasoning to taste.

Meanwhile, cook the tagliatelle in a large pan of boiling salted water until al dente, then drain and add to the pan with the asparagus.

Fold the asparagus into the pasta. Serve with the Pecorino cheese and a drizzle of olive oil.

Crema di asparagi con fragole e briciole croccanti di speck
Cream of asparagus soup with strawberries and speck crumbs

As I was putting these ingredients together for the first time, I wondered if this marriage of flavours would really work. The asparagus with its earthy, slightly salty taste, the strawberries with their sweetness and the savoury crispness of the speck ham ... it all turned out well and I have now repeated it a hundred times.

Serves 6

900g (1¾lb) asparagus spears (white or green)

2 tbsp extra virgin olive oil, plus extra to drizzle

1 garlic clove, peeled and halved

1 potato, peeled and cut into small dice

600ml (1 pint/2½ cups) vegetable stock

6 slices of speck or prosciutto crudo

180g (6oz/generous 1⅓ cup) strawberries, hulled and cut into small pieces, to garnish

salt and freshly ground black pepper

Preheat the oven to 200°C (400°F/Gas 6). Prepare green asparagus by washing it, then bending each spear so it snaps at the point where the woody part begins. Discard the tough, woody base. Prepare white asparagus by cutting away any tough bits at the base of the spears, then using a potato peeler to remove any stringy outer parts.

Heat the olive oil in a pan with the garlic. As soon as the garlic starts to turn golden, add the diced potato and cook for 5 minutes, stirring frequently to ensure it does not stick. Add the prepared asparagus and a little salt (taking into account the saltiness of the stock) and pepper and cook for 7 minutes more.

Meanwhile, bring the stock to the boil in a small pan, then reduce the heat to a simmer. Add the boiling stock, a little at a time, to the pan with the asparagus. Simmer for 15 minutes.

Sandwich the speck or prosciutto crudo between 2 sheets of baking parchment (parchment paper) and put on a baking sheet. Place in the preheated oven and cook for about 10 minutes, until crisp.

Remove the soup from the heat, transfer to a blender and blend until smooth and creamy. Return to the pan and cook for a few minutes more, adding seasoning to taste. Meanwhile, chop the crispy speck into small pieces. Serve the asparagus soup garnished with the chopped strawberries and speck and a drizzle of olive oil.

Asparagi verdi sott'olio con aglio e prezzemolo
Green asparagus in oil with garlic and parsley

Preserving asparagus means that you will always have a great side dish on hand that goes equally well with a plate of really good cured meats, roast meats or just simple boiled eggs.

Serves 6

1kg (2lb) green asparagus

200ml (7fl oz/generous ¾ cup) white wine vinegar

2 garlic cloves, peeled

4 sprigs of flat-leaf parsley

extra virgin olive oil, to cover the asparagus in the jars

salt and coarsely ground white pepper

Wash the asparagus, then bend each spear. The spear should snap easily at the point where the woody part begins. Discard the tough, woody base. Half-fill a tall narrow saucepan with salted water and bring to the boil. Add the vinegar. Stand the asparagus in the pan with their tips just above the boiling water. Cook for 10 minutes. Remove, drain well, dry on a clean cloth and leave to cool.

When cool, stand the asparagus in tall glass jars, tips facing upwards. Add a garlic clove, a little ground white pepper, a few sprigs of parsley and enough olive oil to cover the asparagus. Screw the lids on loosely and leave for a few days.

If the asparagus absorbs some of the oil, add more. Once the asparagus has stopped absorbing oil, screw the lids on tightly and store in a cool, dark place for at least a month before using.

I n these parts we are quite spoiled as regards asparagus and when they are in season we really know how to enjoy them. This delicate, ancient vegetable is something the locals boast about in the Bassano del Grappa area, just a few kilometres from where I live. The white variety grown there has been granted a PDO (Protected Designation of Origin) in recognition of its quality and unique characteristics. However, at the risk of being considered a heretic, I must profess a clear preference for green asparagus though both varieties have exceptional potential in the kitchen; because of their characteristics, either can be used as a base for or an accompaniment to many different dishes. They release an intense aroma when lightly grilled with just a drizzle of oil, but they also combine perfectly with more vigorous tastes like that of Parmesan cheese, and they prove delicious when reduced to an incredibly soft cream offset by the sweet, slightly acid taste of strawberries. Asparagus must, beyond a shadow of doubt, be picked in the right season, when their tips are firm and nicely coloured. They should then be eaten in a really short space of time since they lose moisture and damage quite easily. When that happens, their incomparable sweetness may well be impaired.

Asparagi arrosto con cialda di Parmigiano e vinaigrette al basilico
Asparagus with parmesan crisps and sweet basil dressing

Wonderful as a starter, eye-catching but simple, this dainty dish works well with either white or green asparagus, but I have used white. The Parmesan crisps can be made the day before and kept somewhere cool until ready to serve. Always use the smaller, tender basil leaves.

Serves 6

36 white asparagus spears, tips lightly closed

100ml (3½fl oz/scant ½ cup) extra virgin olive oil, plus extra to drizzle

90g (3½oz) Parmesan cheese shavings

2 tbsp white wine vinegar

10–12 basil leaves, finely sliced

1 small onion, very finely sliced

salt and freshly ground black pepper

Preheat the oven to 190°C (375°F/Gas 5). Prepare the asparagus by cutting away any tough bits at the base of the spears, then using a potato peeler to remove any stringy outer parts.

Arrange the spears in a roasting tin (pan). Drizzle with olive oil, season with salt and pepper, then place in the preheated oven for 8–10 minutes.

Remove the asparagus from the oven. It should be al dente – just cooked but still slightly crisp. Reduce the oven temperature to 160°C (325°F/Gas 3) .

Line a baking sheet with baking parchment (parchment paper) and place 6 tian rings on top. Fill each ring with Parmesan shavings, then place the baking sheet in the oven and cook for 5–6 minutes, until the cheese has melted and started to turn golden brown. Remove from the oven and leave to cool.

Put the remaining oil, the vinegar, a pinch of salt and pepper, and the basil leaves in a bowl. Mix well.

Divide the roasted asparagus spears between 6 plates, top with a few slices of onion and spoon over some dressing. To serve, break the Parmesan crisps in half and arrange on top of the asparagus.

Asparagus

Zabaione al moscato e fragole con biscotti alle mandorle
Zabaione with muscat, strawberries and almond biscuits

For me, this is one of the best custard crème desserts ever. The strawberries temper the richness of the zabaione, and the combination of zabaione and almond biscuits (cookies) gives a pleasing contrast of textures. I can't ever remember any of my friends leaving the tiniest bit.

Serves 6

8 very fresh egg yolks

175g (6oz/generous ¾ cup) caster (superfine) sugar

150ml (¼ pint/scant ⅔ cup) Marsala Cremovo wine

150ml (¼ pint/scant ⅔ cup) Muscat wine

2 pinches of ground cinnamon

600g (1¼lb/generous 4½ cups) strawberries, hulled, dried and cut in small pieces

for the biscuits (cookies)

100g (3½oz/½ cup) caster (superfine) sugar

120g (scant 4oz/½ cup) unsalted butter, softened

1 egg, beaten

100g (3½oz/scant ⅔ cup) almonds, blanched, peeled, toasted and chopped

100g (3½oz/⅔ cup) 00 flour

50g (2oz/⅓ cup) polenta (cornmeal) flour

pinch of salt

zest of ½ lemon, finely grated

25–30 whole almonds, blanched and peeled

icing (confectioners') sugar, for dusting

Start by making the biscuits (cookies). Preheat the oven to 180°C (350°F/Gas 4). In a bowl, combine the sugar and butter and beat until the mixture is soft and smooth. Add the egg and mix together thoroughly. Add the chopped toasted almonds and the 2 flours. Mix well and add the salt and grated lemon zest. Continue mixing until smooth.

Roll a small amount of the mixture into a ball between your fingers, place it on a baking sheet and lightly press a single almond into the top of the ball. Repeat to make 25–30 biscuits (cookies). Place the baking sheet in the preheated oven and cook for 15–18 minutes, until the surface is golden. Cool on a wire rack, then dust with sifted icing (confectioners') sugar.

Preheat the grill (broiler).

Put the egg yolks and sugar in a heatproof bowl and beat together until the mixture is thick and frothy. Add the Marsala and Muscat wines and cinnamon, then cook over a bain-marie, whisking all the time. Remove the pan from the heat as soon as the mixture starts to thicken.

Divide the strawberry pieces between 6 ramekin dishes and pour the zabaione over the top. Put the ramekins under the grill (broiler) and cook until the zabaione has turned a lovely golden colour. Serve hot with the biscuits (cookies) or leave to cool slightly and serve warm.

Fragole al profumo di arance
Orange-spiked strawberries

The spring table would be incomplete without a bowl of strawberries. Their very shape and colour symbolize sweetness. Served imaginatively at the end of a meal, they can rival the most sumptuous cake or pastry.

Serves 6

juice of 2 oranges

2 tbsp raw cane sugar

900g (1¾lb/scant 7 cups) strawberries, hulled

orange zest, finely grated, to decorate

In a large bowl, make a marinade from the orange juice and sugar. Add the strawberries and refrigerate for at least 30 minutes. Serve chilled and decorated with a little orange zest.

Pomodori confit all'aglio fresco
Compote of garlic-scented tomatoes

It is essential to use the very best of the season's red, sweet-smelling, juicy tomatoes for this dish. And don't be afraid of the garlic: you will appreciate its delicate fragrance when it is cooked this way. I will conclude by asking you to use only the very best-quality oil. But you knew that already.

Serves 6

12 just-ripe vine tomatoes, about 150g (5oz) each

700ml (24fl oz/generous 2¾ cups) best-quality extra virgin olive oil

head of garlic, unpeeled

salt

Wash and dry the tomatoes, then slice the base off each so they will stand upright. Heat the olive oil in a shallow pan over a very low heat, add the head of garlic and the tomatoes, then cover and cook for 40 minutes.

The oil must not fry at any stage and when cooked the tomatoes should be very soft but still hold their shape. Add salt to taste and serve.

Zucchine saltate con pinoli e cipollotto
Pan-fried courgettes with pine nuts and spring onions

For a long time pine nuts were associated with southern Italian cooking but today they are everywhere. In this recipe you have, on the one hand, the resinous taste and crunchiness of the pine nuts and on the other, the freshness of taste and delicate texture of the first courgettes (zucchini).

Serves 6

3 tbsp pine nuts

2 tbsp extra virgin olive oil

6 green courgettes (zucchini), with flowers, cut into rounds, flowers reserved

2 spring onions (scallions), thinly sliced

salt and freshly ground black pepper

Heat a dry frying pan over a medium heat, add the pine nuts and toast them, stirring continuously to ensure they do not burn. Set aside.

Heat the olive oil in a frying pan over a medium heat, add the spring onions (scallions) and cook for 2 minutes, until soft.

Add the sliced courgettes (zucchini), together with salt to taste, and cook for 5 minutes, then add the flowers and cook for 2 minutes more. The courgettes (zucchini) should be nice and crisp. Add the toasted pine nuts and a little pepper and stir gently. Serve warm.

Fricassea di agnello e carciofi
Lamb fricassée with globe artichokes

In my opinion, thanks to its base of egg and lemon, this dish is the perfect marriage between the distinct but not overtly strong flavour of lamb and the aromatic and sumptuousness of the artichoke. This recipe is synonymous with Easter in my home. PICTURED ON PAGE 17

Serves 6

6 artichokes

juice of 2 unwaxed lemons

2 tbsp extra virgin olive oil

1kg (2lb) shoulder of lamb, diced

2 garlic cloves, peeled

100ml (3½fl oz/scant ½ cup) dry white wine

3 very fresh egg yolks

salt

a few sprigs of flat-leaf parsley, finely chopped, to garnish

Wash the artichokes, remove the outer leaves and cut them into tiny wedges. Immerse in a bowl of cold water to which you have added 2 tbsp lemon juice. Set aside.

Heat the olive oil in a deep pan over a medium heat. Add the lamb and the garlic and cook for 10–12 minutes, turning occasionally to ensure the meat is golden brown all over and the garlic does not burn. Add salt to taste, increase the heat and add the wine. Continue to cook until the wine has evaporated, then remove the meat to a plate with a slotted spoon and cover with tinfoil to keep warm.

Drain and carefully dry the artichokes, then add to the juices in the pan. Add salt to taste and cook for 5–6 minutes. Return the meat to the pan and continue to cook for 15–20 minutes, until the meat and artichokes are tender.

Put the egg yolks, a pinch of salt and the remaining strained lemon juice in a bowl and mix together.

Remove the lamb from the heat and carefully pour over the egg-yolk mixture, mixing it until the eggs become creamy. Sprinkle with the parsley and serve piping hot.

Brasato di manzo con le verdure
Italian pot roast

I really love this recipe. It is the perfect dish when time is short and dinner guests are many. It is even tastier when prepared well in advance, but if you can't manage that, simply make it in the morning for the evening.

PICTURED ON PAGE 16

Serves 6

1.2kg (2½lb) best pot-roasting steak (topside [round] or chuck)

40ml (scant 2fl oz/scant ¼ cup) extra virgin olive oil

2 garlic cloves, crushed

75ml (3fl oz/scant ⅓ cup) dry white wine

500ml (17fl oz/2 cups) light vegetable stock, plus extra if needed

4 sage leaves, chopped

2–3 sprigs of thyme

300g (10oz) small new potatoes, peeled

4 courgettes (zucchini), cut into chunks

4 spring onions (scallions), cut into chunks

2 carrots, peeled and cut into chunks

2 celery sticks, cut into chunks

salt and freshly ground black pepper

If the butcher has not already done so, roll and tie the meat. Heat the olive oil in a large flameproof casserole dish over a medium heat. Add the meat and garlic and fry, turning occasionally, until the meat is golden brown all over. Increase the heat, add the wine and continue to cook until the wine has evaporated, then add the hot stock, sage and thyme. Season to taste with salt and pepper, cover, reduce the heat and cook for 30 minutes more. Add more stock if necessary.

Add the potatoes, courgettes (zucchini), spring onions (scallions), carrots and celery to the casserole dish and cook for 1 hour more.

When ready to serve, untie the meat and cut into slices. Serve the meat piping hot with the vegetables and the pan juices.